MR HARTY'S
Grand Tour

MR HARTY'S
Grand Tour

· Russell Harty ·

Illustrated by
Jane Lake Birt

CENTURY
LONDON MELBOURNE AUCKLAND JOHANNESBURG

First published in 1988 by Century Hutchinson Ltd
Brookmount House, 62–65 Chandos Place, Covent Garden
London WC2N 4NW

Century Hutchinson Australia Pty Ltd
PO Box 496, 16–22 Church Street, Hawthorn, Victoria 3122
Australia

Century Hutchinson New Zealand Ltd
PO Box 40–086, Glenfield, Auckland 10
New Zealand

Century Hutchinson South Africa Pty Ltd
PO Box 337 Bergvlei
2012 South Africa

Typeset by SX Composing Ltd, Essex
Printed and Bound in Great Britain by
Butler and Tanner Ltd, Frome and London

ISBN 0 7126 1849 X

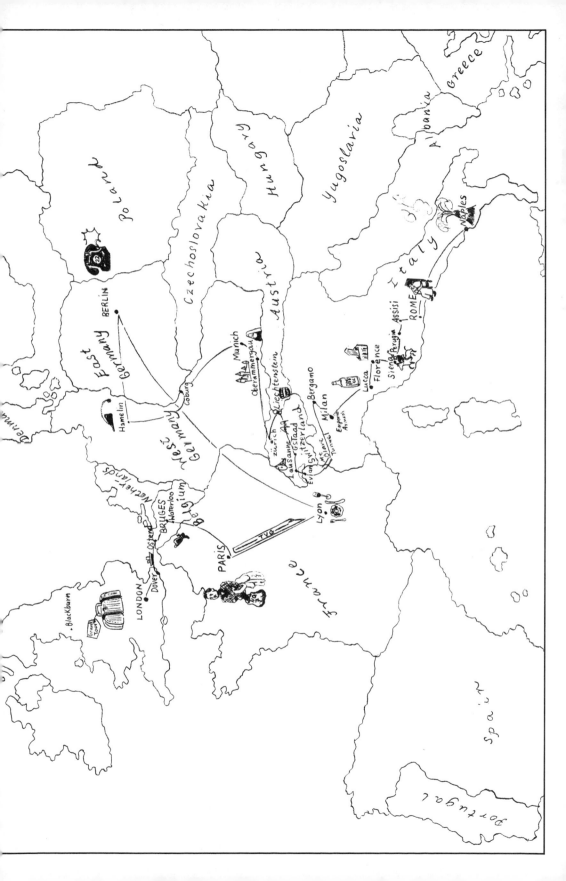

CHAPTER
ONE

I wish I could be more enthusiastic about Paris. It catches
me on the wrong foot. The problem is mainly historical.
I was scarred and scared at too early an age. Paris was the
first place I ever went to 'abroad'.

'I think,' I announced to the family round the fire, one
night, in the wet zones of post-war Blackburn, 'I think I
should have a French pen-friend.'

'Don't talk daft,' my mother said.

'Good idea,' said my more venturesome father.

'What I thought was . . . (swallow) that I would put an
advert in *The Times* and ask if there was anyone in Paris who
would like to come to Blackburn for an improving stay, and
then I could go back to Paris and polish my French.'

'Good idea,' said my venturesome father, the man who
introduced the avocado to Blackburn.

'Don't talk daft,' said my mother, her mind filled with the
dolorous helium of domestic responsibility. Her mind-
computer was already churning with the problems of clean
sheets, a new set of cups and saucers, and the awesome prospect of having to invest in a clove of garlic. Some kind of
commonsense prevailed and an advertisement was placed in
the Personal Columns of *The Times*.

'Young Englishman . . . Parisian . . . exchange . . . language . . .' The usual. The word 'Parisian' is interesting in this context. I think I can safely claim that I had not heard of Bordeaux or Lyon. Paris, yes. The zest and the singular identity of the place quite overwhelmed any other place in post-war Europe. It is in the nature of the capital city to draw to itself all the magnetic properties of 'abroad'. You can drink all day – the fundamental attraction in a licence-bound land. Gaulloises, wine, Piaf, and those blue and white striped sailors who dragged blousy women from a bar table and apache-danced themselves into a brutal but sexually powerful insensitivity. These were the hidden and forbidden identifications of the city. Further to the front, revealed, and therefore less intriguing, were the Eiffel Tower, the Louvre, the Mona Lisa, the bouquinistes, the bateaux mouches . . .

Imagine, then, the considerable joy when a letter with a French postmark was delivered to the doormat some two weeks after the appearance of the advert. The engagement was made. He was to visit me in the August. I was to go to him, and his family, at Christmas.

He arrived at Blackburn Railway Station on 10 August 1952. The family, in its ill-fitting finery, formed a welcoming party on the platform. He was one of the last to get off the train, and he was unmistakeable. Tall, composed, suited, and carrying just the one case. This casual lightness of travel attracted my mother's critical attention. 'If he's here for three weeks, how can he be carrying everything in that small case?' His command of the English language was less confident than mine of the French.

'Je veux vous introduire à mon père, ma mère, et ma soeur, Saundra.'

This was easy. I had rehearsed it, in and out of the days and nights preceding his arrival. He tried to kiss my mother's hand, but she became confused and pretended that none of this was happening. We drove home. There was a sensible English tea waiting for him. Thick slices of ham, a tasteless salad, with slivers of hard-boiled egg tastefully arranged on the summit of the greenery. No hint of dressing. No black pepper. Everything sensible and inoffensive.

It had to be this way round. By that, I mean that if I had gone to Paris before he came to Lancashire, it would have been impossible to discharge my obligation.

★   ★   ★

I am sitting now in the Café Deux Magots, in the Boulevard St Germain, with a glass of white wine and a 'croque monsieur' – toasted ham and cheese, which sounds dull in English but tastes good in France. Paris has, over the years, reduced me to minimal activity. There are two or three hotels in the 6th arrondisement which I patronise with a certain pleasure. I do not feel the need to venture further since I am comfortably accommodated in this area. The place is a jumble of artists dressed like artists, smart old ladies with tired old dogs, young models, fashionable men who could be bankers or librarians or bin collectors, and a diminishing straggle of American back-packers, in wire glasses, looking for the shade of Mr Hemingway.

The wine is served straight away, by an efficient and unenthusiastic serving machine, a little moustache, a long white apron, and no desire to look you in the face and, perhaps, give you the odd smile. He is not hostile. He gets the order correct but there is little evidence of warmth or personal pleasure.

'I think, maybe, we ordered some more croques monsieur, monsieur,' I say in over-pronounced, mildly exaggerated French. He nods in quick understanding, but is already taking someone else's order.

All the guide books of Paris say that one of the capital's chief assets is its pavement cafés, where you sit for a lingering drink and examine the world as it passes the window. I am not sure that this is an accurate reading. I am much more aware of the passers-by examining me. They stare in a quizzical, almost critical, fashion. They slow down their step when they reach the corner of the Deux Magots. The café windows become a sort of fish tank. The passers-by become, in effect, the audience, and you, the visiting customer, appear almost trapped behind the proscenium glass.

There is an interesting way of coping with this situation, taught to me many years ago by an old friend. It is a method whereby you can relieve yourself of the embarrassment of being stared at, and also play the liveliest of naughty games with the passer-by. So, here comes the croque monsieur, and another glass of wine, merci, and the atmosphere begins to warm a little. The alcohol, in its mildest form, gives courage and confidence to your pronunciation of the French language, and, maybe, Paris isn't so full of prohibitive chic as you'd thought. Time to start the game, which is both simple and silly.

'You have to spend the night with the seventh person who walks past the window from left to right. OK?'

There's something in this farrago to suit everybody, except the poor unwitting devil who happens to be the seventh past the window. There are amusing variations, too. You don't have to spend the night. It could be half an hour, or the rest of your life. You don't have to be in Paris to play this game, either. Except that the variety and the reliably moving stream of pedestrians along the Boulevard St Germain offer the best possible circumstance for general joy. Look at the astonishment in the face of this elegantly coiffed madame. She is taking a haughty lunch-time stroll, with her whitely-dyed chihuahua tucked under her arm. And when she has finished staring, in mild disdain, at your croque monsieur, she registers the fact that you and your companion are consumed with mirth, and a mirth which, somehow, she seems to have inspired. It's rather like sniggering at someone who has wiped an eye with a sooty finger. Madame hurries her step so that she can discreetly check her face or her figure. She wouldn't have enjoyed the night, anyway. Her hair took too long to arrange. She wouldn't permit any form of human untidiness.

When the fun has evaporated from this game, and a small cup of black coffee is served, I allow my imagination to wander back home, back to that unnerving first evening of Étienne's visit to Blackburn. The leisure time that travel provides, these moments of coffee-flavoured recollection, when you're not rushing to pack, or queuing in a tetchy line waiting to be frisked, often throw up the strangest thoughts. Somewhere, a street or two away from this café, perhaps a respectably middle-aged Étienne is rehearsing the details of his first nightmare visit to Britain. Who knows? And who, indeed, knows whether he would remember it as I do?

★　　★　　★

We had finished our family tea by half-past six. When I say 'tea' I mean a substantial meal, not something with small biscuits and a pot of lapsang souchong. In those days, the television service did not start to broadcast until eight o'clock, and, in any case, we were still enslaved to the wireless and its instant homely variety. No self-respecting Northern family would consider the idea of not having a coal fire in the hearth, even at the height of mid-summer. So, after tea, we sat around the fire, in a strained circle, my father lightly perspiring in his suit jacket and clearly thinking that an entire month of this formal family behaviour would send him to the dark edge of sanity. The house was unusually quiet. Normally, there were violent quarrels about the simplest of things. 'Who left that sideboard door open?' 'Somebody has put a cup on this table, and there's a nasty ring on the woodwork.' That was the normal level of family conversation. The simplest things exploded into fiery volcanoes of argument, often ending in silly and petulant silences, which could last half an hour . . . or the whole night. The same arbitrary measurement of time which one used when playing the game at the Deux Magots.

Étienne was given the second best chair, on the other side of the fireplace from my father. My mother, my sister and I sat, like figures from a primitive Northern painting, in a line on the sofa. I couldn't think of anything to say. We listened to the wireless. Laughed a little. My father offered the *Blackburn Evening Telegraph* to our French visitor, who used it in the strangest way, and raised the worst suspicions in one's mind. He had, somehow, managed to smuggle in a bag of French chocolates and had stuffed them down the side of the chair. Whenever the *Evening Telegraph* trembled a little, you could hear him scrabbling in the bag and then juicily munching these delicacies behind the paper. This, as you can imagine, did not go down at all well. We had been taught to share everything, and, if necessary, to offer the last toffee to the house guest. Here was this stranger, not been in the house for two hours, our guest, given a proper tea, now sitting in front of the fire helping himself, if you please, to a bag of French delights. And making no effort to pass them round. Really! A network of suspicious looks passed between the rest of us. This did not bode well. But things took a vastly different turn half an hour later.

'Perhaps Étienne would like to look at some of our books of the Royal Family?' suggested my mother, keeping her annoyance under control. My father was already sliding towards sleep. When Étienne had finished his surreptitious munching, he put down the paper and came to sit in the middle of the sofa. It never, of course, occurred to me, at this stage, and with one vast Sahara of a month ahead of him, that he might just be thinking to himself that he had landed the worst deal of his young life. Egg and cress for tea, followed by a night sitting round the fire, reading the Births, Marriages and Deaths column in the local paper and rounding off a jolly family party inspecting a pile of books about the British Royal Family.

'Ici Le Roi George, et sa femme, La Reine Elizabeth, dans votre cité de Paris,' I pronounced carefully, pointing at a photograph taken on a recent state visit to post-war France by our then King and Queen.

'Oui,' he replied, without any apparent interest, 'et ça, c'est mon père.' He pointed to a tall and distinguished figure standing to one side of the King.

I started to explain the same picture again. 'Er . . . ceci . . . cet homme is notre roi, King George le Sixième.'

'Oui.'

'Et sa femme s'appelle Elizabeth. En anglais, nous disons "Queen Elizabeth".'

'Oui.'

'What's he saying?' my mother half-whispered, the memory of the chocolates still uppermost in her affronted conscience.

'I don't quite know what he's thinking,' I replied truthfully, at this stage sensing only the distant and unpleasant possibility of my leg being pulled.

'Leurs majestés étaient dans votre cité de Paris!' Why I had to keep on telling him that his own city was called Paris, I do not know.

'Oui, et ça, c'est mon père,' he repeated.

'Père?'

'Oui, mon père.' There was no mistaking his meaning. Just the accuracy of his preposterous claim. My mother caught the scent of silent panic.

'Well, he says that this man, here, is his father. The man behind the King.'

My father shifted uneasily in his half-sleep.

'Don't be daft,' huffed my mother. 'His father? How can it be his father? I thought you were supposed to understand some French.'

There was, at this moment, a cloud no bigger than a man's hand, looming ominously upon the horizon of this evening's activities. Had one, perhaps, entered upon an engagement which was going to destroy us all? Was this young chocolate-eating whipper-snapper playing silly buggers? Were we being taken for a royal ride? Was he laughing at us? Tormenting us?

'Mon père,' he explained calmly, 'est le Chef de Protocol du Président Auriol.'

I was now too intoxicated with this intelligence to deal with the simplicity of its message. 'Chef', in any case, meant only one thing at that time. So that I became even more confused by the description of his father's position.

'Mon père a organisé les détails de la visite,' he added, turning a page with nonchalance.

'What I think he is saying,' I announced as flatly as my fluttering response would allow, 'is that his father works for the French President and organised this French visit.'

'Oui. Ça. Vous avez raison.'

There is a delicious line in a play written by Alan Bennett. A Chinese waiter, looking for his girlfriend, finds himself by mistake in a hospital ward. He has a box of chocolates (wouldn't you know?) which he wants to give her, to woo her with. He can't find her, so in benign Oriental manner, he leaves the box for an old, rambling patient, who is lying in the next bed to the majestic Thora Hird. She scents chocolate, and bounces out of her cot to seize the sweets and to make a characteristically Northern dismissal of the mix-up.

'It will take,' she says, already chewing a Turkish Delight and searching for an Orange cream, 'it will take more than a box of Dairy Milk to wipe out the memory of Pearl Harbor!'

I know where that line came from. I know how quickly a character can be transformed. It doesn't need anything so obvious as an ass's head. Bless thee, Bottom, how art thou translated! A rather loutish chocolate-eating frog had suddenly changed into a handsome French Prince.

'Perhaps Étienne would like a glass of sherry?' enquired a now solicitous mother. Sherry, indeed. Sherry, a bottle of sweet, dark sherry, was kept for those important occasions when a child was christened or a grandmother died and an unctuous vicar came to make arrangements in the cold front room.

'I'm sure Étienne would like to meet Auntie Annie and Uncle Fred. And Auntie Celia, maybe. Just waken your father and tell him a few people are coming round for a drink.'

It took a time to explain everything to my wakened father. Nobody had ever been to our house for a drink. Not on a Tuesday. There was a moment, in this hastily convened and hysterically conducted party, when it seemed as though madness might finally overtake us all and the bottle of maraschino cherries, bought years ago for no reason, might finally be opened in order to grace the rim of a cocktail glass.

★   ★   ★

Supposing the seventh person to pass this window, here in the Deux Magots, were to be . . .!

The time for recollection of temps mercifully perdu had, however, passed; and I left the dream corner house in order to meet a gentleman who has had an inordinately powerful influence on my life as a traveller. He works in an anonymous building in an anonymous quartier of Paris. He is the Director of all those anonymous men and women who scour Europe in the service of the Michelin guides. I mean the Red Guides, which take time to understand. Books full of the strange hieroglyphs of a language which makes the traveller's lot easier, more comfortable, cheaper even. The Michelin Guide exerts the most hypnotic fascination, once you are party to its secrets; and, once you become easily acquainted with its private sign language, it is the most reliable of companions. It makes no demands, and responds, almost clinically, to nearly all of yours.

I had expected M. le Directeur to be an expansive figure who might offer a glass of wine. He was an austere, sombre, rather a diffident customer. We met in a large bare room. He sat at one end of a long, empty table, fingers locked, staring icily through his directorial glasses and uncomfortable at the thought that someone would spring a surprise question. Power occasionally manifests itself in odd forms. In my naïveté, I had imagined a rather papal figure, the size, say, of an abbot, who knew how to live well, eat and drink with relish. Perhaps a dictatorial figure, sitting in a grand red chair with a large quill pen, behaving in the manner of a cultivated Mussolini, bestowing his crossed knives and forks to this eating house, and in a secret consistory, with bells tolling and a choir filling the air with an Epicurean anthem, bestowing a rosette upon a blushing chef. Make no mistake. These are important commercial awards. A red rosette or a red rocking chair can change the life of a proprietor overnight. Here will now be a place well worth the detour. Here you can expect excellence, and not always at a price. The corollary is barely to be contemplated. If you lose a rosette, you may as well put your head into the gas oven where formerly rose a light and delicious soufflé.

Nothing persuasively human came back to me by way of response. I asked him whether he knew that there were certain people who were more concerned about their Red Guide than they were about their passport. He simply nodded. In the end, I came to understand that I was prolonging his personal agony. He is, after all, the repository of much important individual and private information. One of the reasons for the superiority of the Michelin is this grand anonymity. There is no gossip. No hint of a personal influence. Not the remotest possibility of corruption. At the end of the day, the reliability of the guide is founded upon harsh rules, and M. le Directeur was in no mood to satisfy my desire for the current gossip.

It was nearly lunchtime and I thought it quite a legitimate question to ask him whether there was a restaurant in the neighbourhood which he could personally recommend.

'You have a copy of the guide at hand,' he said. 'If you study it carefully, you will find the answer to that question there.'

It was time to move on. Thank you. Clicked heels. Cold hand shake. Bonjour.

★　　★　　★

Some years ago, I was invited to present a radio programme from Paris. It was an early edition of a chat programme called *Midweek*. We were looking for guests who were able to conduct a cheerful conversation in English but for whom Paris was either home, or work. There was a new British Ambassador, lately installed in the large, elegant house in the Rue du Faubourg St Honoré. He was Sir John Fretwell and it was said, amongst polite but gossipy circles, that his wife, Mary, did a lot of their personal shopping at the new Marks & Spencer in Paris. I asked her to join the group of guests to talk about her life and her work in the plum diplomatic posting. She agreed, rather cheerfully, and we became friends. We had, as I remember, a difficult moment at the start of that Wednesday morning programme. We were sitting in a studio, an odd mix of people who included another now good friend, Myrtle Allen of Ballymaloe House in Ireland. She is a restaurateuse of great distinction, suitably garlanded by Michelin, and she had just opened an eating house in Paris. Danielle in the lion's (or Lyon's) den. She called it La Ferme Irlandaise and, in those days, it served soda bread, Kerry butter, salmon from the Shannon, game from the Knockmealdown Mountains, and home-made black puddings. Just before we went on the air, there was a news flash which announced that Princess Grace, Grace Kelly, had been killed in a road accident, in Monte Carlo. In those days, one was too nervous to respond quickly and intelligently to such an emotional moment. There were three or four of us round the table who knew Princess Grace, and it was such a shocking and unexpected moment, that one was grateful for the diplomatic calm signalled by Mary Fretwell.

'Shall we talk about this?' I enquired.

'I think not,' said Lady Fretwell, with an official British voice which left nor need nor reason for further debate.

In the hey-day of the Grand Tourist, it was almost a matter of obligation to call upon the Ambassador, present your card, declare your intentions, and expect to receive assistance to reach otherwise forbidden places. He, for instance, could help you to assist at the levée of the Roi Soleil. From all contemporary accounts, it seems that the world and his wife and a considerable amount of children would make the journey out to Versailles, to watch the monarch's teeth being cleaned, and to see him eat a morning orange.

★　　★　　★

Any passing psychiatrist would have little difficulty in noting that I am, in many ways, a snob. I look at the way people hold their knives and forks and pretend to know from what sort of background they spring. This is because, at a dinner party, one night many years ago, shortly after I became a schoolmaster, my hostess pointed out that one of her obligations, as a housemaster's wife, was to teach the Sixth Form how to behave decently at table. And that included the proper holding of the knife and fork. That there was, indeed, a certain way, considered presentable, had never occurred to me. For twenty-three years, I had cradled my fork, comfortably, between the index finger and the thumb of my right hand. 'For instance,' said my hostess, 'members of the working classes always seem to cradle their fork between the thumb and index finger.'

I only need lightning to strike like that once in order to illuminate the social landscape and reveal me in the flash of disadvantage. I slithered the offending instrument out of its customary, comfortable cleft and have, thereafter, placed the index finger along the top of the blade. What, I wonder, do the Chinese working class do with their chopsticks? It's the sort of thing that doesn't matter unless it matters. Then, it matters a great deal.

It was about the same disturbing time that I tried to rearrange my pronunciation. As well as being a snob, I am also a chameleon, and, for a certain peace of mind and in order to merge into the landscape, I will try to imitate the prevailing accent of the company. If you're using the word 'one', then one will use it. If I am with old school mates who speak still in their native dialect, I will exaggerate my vowels accordingly. It is a dreary and patronising way of behaving, but after so long a time practising such social deceit, it has become second nature. The problem is, one forgets what one's first nature is. I am frequently tripped by it. 'Push', 'sugar', 'bush', 'butcher', and 'pudding' are small but dangerous mines in life's otherwise plain path.

I was infected at an impressionable age by Nancy Mitford's harmless but penetrating judgments of those who knew or were non-U. I snear at the word 'toilet' and shock the genteel by my use of the lavatory. But then I get lost in the looking glass, and can't remember if I should call you back, or wait until you 'phone me. It is absurd, but, for me, not uninteresting.

Brewer's Dictionary of Phrase and Fable says that 'snob' is a shortened form of the Latin words *sine nobilitate . . .* without the attributes of noble birth. But just as you have accommodated yourself to that simple explanation, and you turn to the *Longman Dictionary of Word Origins* to make quite sure, you discover that 'snob' means a 'vulgar and ostentatious person', and that the word is derived from the Old English dialect for 'shoemaker'.

This shoemaker without noble ancestry would write a note to Her Britannic Majesty's Ambassador in Paris, to inform him of one's intention to call, in passing through the city in the course of a Grand Tour. Mary Fretwell wrote an unsnobbish reply inviting me to lunch, and suggesting that it might be a reasonable idea to invite one or two guests to join us. This would, perhaps, serve to divert the passing hour.

In the olden days, you could knock on the large wooden doors of the Embassy, tell the porter that you had business with His Excellency, and then be ushered through. In this late part of the twentieth century, an open house is only opened if you can penetrate your official way in. The British Embassy is a part of that smart and expensive neighbourhood in which the French President has his official residence. (The Elysée Palace.) There are barriers along the length of the street and pedestrians must walk along the opposite side. There are guards patrolling for twenty-four hours of every day, and each one has a primed pistol which he is trained to use. You might think it the safest place in the world. But in fact, it is not. You could be mugged, raped or murdered in that street and no guard would come to your assistance. It might be a ruse to entice him away from his post. If you stand across the street from our Embassy and look closely at the upper parts of the buildings, you will see cameras strategically positioned to observe your comings and goings. The Ambassador may now only extend his hospitality to those who can pass, in every way, through the tightest screens of security.

Once inside, you would know none of this. At the large glass door at the top of the front steps, you (or one) is received by a footman and a butler. One (or you) has (have) no need to say who you are. That is all silently taken care of. 'Your coat, sir.' 'Perhaps you would care to wash your hands?' 'Would you kindly step this way?' The grand staircase, which leads from the marble hallway and the state rooms, up to the drawing-room and the dining-room, seems to me to be set as a deliberate architectural test. The steps are polished to a dangerously icy gloss. Ascending is easier than descending. When you go up, you can, as it were, drag yourself step by step and hold on to the balustrade. Coming down means you have carefully to seek out each step as though it were a safe shelf for a moment of self-collecting steadiness. One is, in any case, trying to keep oneself balanced upon the nervous edge of best behaviour.

The most interesting and immediate impressions are those of smell. The first time I was there, the air was filled with the mixed scents of hyacinths and burning cherry wood. If you closed your eyes and drifted a little, you could have spirited yourself to the Cotswolds on a spring day. On the Tour, I arrived there at lilac time. It is no ordinary lilac. The blossom is heavy-headed, almost overladen, and sending out a powerful aroma. A gin and tonic, an exquisite dog, a deep and relaxing sofa, a deeper and even more relaxing cigarette, and you begin to feel the problems of state security or personal pronunciation, gently evaporating. The snob bobs to the surface. Look around you. You could have been born for such special circumstance. You cannot help but feel like a Grand Tourist.

A footman announces the arrival of Monsieur Rudolf Nureyev, and he materialises. Smaller and more twinkling than I had remembered. There comes a time in most people's lives when confidence makes them more comfortable companions. Nureyev used to be a terribly prickly customer. I think in the time immediately after his defection from Mother Russia, and, particularly, at that period of his life when he was living in the harsh fastidious glare of audiences and critics, that he was a difficult character to share a table or a studio with. Things here and now are altogether different. Nureyev is the Director of the Paris Ballet and even though there are headaches about bookings, and engagements, and arrangements for travel, and the constant bitchings of the internecine battles of any ballet company, and worry about a possible return to Russia, now accomplished: despite all these preoccupations, he is good company.

No sooner do we sit down to chew a little old fat, and to shred a few reputations, than the footman returns to announce the arrival of Miss Charlotte Rampling. She too is smaller and more cheerful than I had remembered. What is happening? Is everybody shrinking? Am I getting taller, or fatter? Or do the surroundings of the Embassy, in part domestic, in part almost theatrical, make everyone appear different?

Sir John Fretwell is at pains to point out that life in the British Embassy is not one long and elegant lunch party. True, the Visitors' Book, on the great table in the hall, places this house firmly in the living and flowing history of contemporary France. Practically every member of the Royal Family claims bed and breakfast. It is, after all, her Britannic Majesty's Embassy. The Union Jack flies over the building, and, legally, that plot of land and its garden, and the next door Chancellery, belong to Britain. Though if relations with France were suddenly to turn sour and the Euro-tunnel blocked off, I doubt whether the house could withstand a lengthy siege. In such a miserable eventuality, it would mean that Habitat, and Marks & Spencer, and W. H. Smith, would also have capitulated, and life, as it is now lived, would be much less cosmopolitan. Though at the snobbish back of my mind, I have to cleave to the faltering conviction that one does not go to live in Paris in order to be near C & A.

In the same Visitors' Book, there are the signatures of many more Trades Union officials than members of the Royal Family. The Ambassador must now spend a large part of his working day, and as much diplomatic influence as he has, promoting the commercial prosperity of Britain. Endless trade fairs, informed conversations with the earnest manufacturers of shoes (or snobs, as they used to be called), delegates from Manchester who will wish to talk well into the early hours about the importance of a certain weave of textile, cheese exporters, red-nosed Scottish lairds pressing the fluid claims of their local whisky . . .

This morning, Sir John has been necessarily cheerful and suitably concerned about the British Wool Secretariat. A gin and tonic is a suitable reward for such service. Lady Fretwell, after a private session with her own horse at the École Militaire, nodding to the odd passing Générale and savouring the enjoyment and the privilege that comes the way of any sensible Ambassador's wife, turns her attention to the kitchen freezer. Since she is the mistress of the house, she is responsible for its linen sheets and its chair covers and, in consultation with the chef, the daily menus – be it a private lunch, like today's, or a state banquet for the French Prime Minister, as last week. Even the best British intentions of an Ambassadress can be frustrated. She had ordered a large quantity of grouse to be shipped over and stored in the deep freeze. A useful national dish on a French state occasion. But the grouse aren't shifting. The chef is not delirious about the prospect of over-ripe foreign birds. The freezer is too harsh. Still, not to complain too much, when there is fresh pâté, and the morning's market salad.

However skilful a hostess you may be, and however careful and attentive a host, even if you are placed in such an elegant context as this house once owned by Pauline Borghese, Napoleon's sister, there is no way in the world that you can legislate for the success of any particular party. Nureyev, Rampling, the Fretwells and me (or I). What have we in common? They all live and work in Paris. They aren't passing through. They are not tourists seeking diversion and entertainment on what is likely to be a long and exhausting haul. There is no one you can ring or 'phone to ask how to play it, and how they think it will go. There is no library which houses a book of reference which will guarantee some kind of positive satisfaction in an undertaking of this sort. There is, I dare bet, no consultant crystal ball gazer who could have foretold that, by the time we retired to the garden room, to drink coffee, smoke a cigarette, sip a liqueur, we would then have found ourselves gratifyingly entangled in an argument about earth burial or cremation. Lady Fretwell is trying to get permission to be laid to rest in a corner of the Embassy garden. Rampling is not the least bit worried where she is flung. I change my mind with each passing persuasion. The conversation, although it smacks most profoundly of departure and death and our final commital to the fire or to the worms, is not remotely morbid. Perhaps you can only lift off into speculations of mortality if you have been suitably inoculated against the long littleness of life by good food, good wine and a quicksilver company.

It is surprising, though, how quickly you can be transformed from the ethereal to the vulgarly mundane. As this lunch was drawing to a conclusion, I observed Mary Fretwell searching under the table for the remote control of an electric bell which would summon the servants to prepare for our departure.

And, in a flash, I was back in the old Paris, suffering the indignities of a spotty and insecure adolescent. Étienne, this seminal Parisian influence, haunted even this particular feast with his spectral presence.

★ ★ ★

When he had, with apparent relief, left Blackburn Railway Station with a best-dressed family waving fond farewells and making doubly sure that the ill-chosen presents would be properly delivered to his semi-royal family, his final words, not uttered with boundless enthusiasm, were that he would look forward to receiving me during the next Christmas holiday. And I, poor fool, believed him, and could not make the time gallop too swiftly towards this splendid appointment. There were, then, no warning bells, no dreadful tocsin sounding a note of caution.

I arrived at the Gare du Nord. I had travelled in what Baedeker used to call 'grand confort et luxe'.

'We don't want our Russell arriving third class, do we! We have to do it properly. They'll all be there, lined up, like we were. There's this proper train called the Golden Arrow. He can go on that. It'll cost us a lot of money. But these people are important.'

I arrived in a flurry of nerves. New suit. Luggage that contained enough clothes to last half a lifetime. New and pinching shoes. A complete blackout about the French language. God knows that in this strange journey, abroad for the first time, and alone, I had had enough time to rehearse and to re-rehearse my greetings. But all I could concentrate on was trying to conjugate the subjunctive mood. Whenever would I need to use it? The Lancastrian answer is that you never know when it might come in handy. And that particular warning, for all I know, might well be an illustration of the subjunctive mood at work.

There was no one there at the Gare du Nord. I dragged my suitcase off the train and did my best to fend off the anxious porters who wanted to conduct me, at presumably a King's ransom, to my rendezvous at the barrier. I stood under the vast clock, disaffected, dispossessed, lost in a strange land where everybody talked as swiftly as they moved, and silently cursed the whole wretched enterprise. Travel, you begin to realise, isn't all it's cracked up to be. How many times, in how many ports, airports, railway stations, have I fallen upon the debilitating conclusion that the whole thing has been a dreadful mistake. This was the first, and most painful, time. When the main flow of well-heeled Golden Arrow passengers had passed through the vast cavern of the station, a young French man, with a bored friend, sauntered over.

'You are Mr Russell?'

'Oui, I am,' I replied in part relief, part anxiety.

'I am the brother of Étienne. He is not here. He has engagement. I take you home.'

At least someone to take care of me. But not someone I knew or understood. We travelled quickly through wet December streets. I was in the back of the car. The two lads,

21 years old, I would guess, and, therefore, well out of my teenage-range, chattered and laughed incessantly. No reference was made to me. And I could not interrupt with my dullish French platitudes. We swung through large gates and into the courtyard of the town house. The brother showed a distant hint of good grace and offered to carry my suitcase. I watched incredulity collect at the corners of his mouth when he felt the embarrassing weight of my case. The obverse of the situation with Étienne and his little valise. I had, by this time, made firm plans to clear out of this city as soon as I could arrange it with some dignity.

The house was as grand as I had begun to fear. There were two aged servants. One opened and closed the doors; the other took delivery of the case from Étienne's brother and dragged the lump up the stairs, to lead me to my room. I had never before heard of anyone unpacking a case, and this man, a complete stranger, was already taking out those private articles of clothing best left unseen. Eventually, and nervously, I made my way to the drawing-room. I was introduced to the Chef de Protocol and Madame. They both behaved with a certain Proustian distraction. I recall an ocean of chintz, polished wooden floors and a sweep of lace curtains. No one made an effort to show me picture books of the French presidents. I was left very much to my own devices. Étienne did not appear until breakfast the next day. There was little warmth in his handshake, and little enthusiasm in his suggestion that we should take a quick trip around the city.

The lid blew off on Christmas Eve. The siege of Paris began. It was, as the French call it, 'un cauchemar'. We were summoned to Midnight Mass at the grand church of St Sulpice. There we foregathered in the family pew to witness the first minutes of the morning of Christ's nativity. It was an impressive ritual, and, to my impressionable eye, maybe more so than it sounds. This ceremony was in the final and arrogantly secure days just before Vatican II. The altar of this high church securely clamped to the East end, no embarrassing suggestions of a faltering handshake with a near neighbour, and, as yet, no suspicion of a pretendedly meaningful kiss of peace. Each celebrant in his rightful place, and a place for every celebrant. The priests robed in surplices of white and gold; the choir in jubilant mood; an organ thundering to shake the earth; the smell of incense to remind you that, as the earth was shaking, the heavens were telling the glory of God. There was not, even to my amazed witness, any sign of a home-made crib, any suggestion of toy animals, sand, chickenwire, and all the diminishing impediments of currently enlightened religious principle. The Word was made flesh, that midnight clear, in a haze of superstitious wonder. For me, that is.

We walked home, the family chattering, me in a mood of high exaltation, not analysing what I had been a part of, but knowing, deep in the cold bone, that something important had come to pass. Sadly, the protection and safety of this mystical feeling did not last too long. We came into the warmth of the great sitting-room, where, would you believe, they did not have a matching three-piece suite. Just the odd chairs and some spindly but 'important' (as Sotheby's would now call them) sofas. No coal fires, not even a log fire: just the distant hum of an antique central heating system, which pounded through the house like the pipes and radiators of a Northern classroom.

We drank champagne and wished each other a happy Christmas, and everybody kissed everybody else, and so did I, after the second glass. Then, as subsequently so often, my position shifted from that of a disturbed spectator, to that of a not-unwilling player. At dinner, I was invited to swallow my first oyster. Emboldened now by the life-enhancing quality of the champagne, I swallowed with the rest and the best of them. Even I had made a clear note that I seemed to be placed in an honourable position by the right-hand side of Étienne's mother. He was sitting somewhere down the side of the long table, far away. His choice, I now suppose. He must have registered his boredom with this mistake of an exchanged provincial lump whose only requirements were to see the *Mona Lisa* and ride up the Eiffel Tower. Even now my hand is damp with the shame of it all.

The early morning, for now it was half-past one o'clock, when any sensible gentleman of England might properly expect to be a-bed, seemed to be roaringly successful. Yes, I will have another glass. Yes, the oysters were delicious. No, we don't have an English equivalent of this feast. The Réveillon, is it? Yes . . . In England, we would be sleeping in preparation for our Christmas lunch, or peepingly half-awake in order not to miss the visit of Father Christmas.

Madame surveyed the table and determined that it was time to organise the next course – a course of action which, by one or two simple movements, caused the plates to be removed, and at the same time, catapulted me, with one or two slight adjustments of Madame's hand into confusion.

She put out her right hand and started to fiddle underneath the table, near to my left thigh. I stared ahead. I felt her hand lightly brush my knee. I kept staring. She seemed to be investigating the geography of my lower body. My brain, charged with the powerful fume of champagne, a fermentation more immediate than the sweet sherry we had poured into Étienne last August, churned with a thrilling suspicion. The delicate touch of a native hand – might it translate an inexperienced pubescent into an internationally accomplished – how shall I say this? – into a knowing young man?

And how should I respond? Her clear face, occupied with the social affairs of dinner, betrayed nothing of the subterranean explorations. She wasn't fooling me, though. I had seen artistically naughty French films before. Films in which a Signoret or a Moreau would make or mar (or both) the young and innocent gardener before his violent exclusion from Eden. Should I yield my knee? Could the others tell that the rising levels of scarlet in otherwise pale cheeks was nought to do with the toxic effects of oysters, and all to do with the imminent loss of innocence? If I ignored her, or moved prudently to another position, perhaps I would be thrown into the street.

She found the hidden electric bell, under the table, near my shaking knee. She pressed it, giving me a sidelong smile. The oysters were transported. And I was deposited back upon real earth, with a dull sublunary thud.

★   ★   ★

That was more or less the end of my first miserable visit to the French capital. It was a visit, as I have indicated, that has

coloured every subsequent Parisian experience. And it confirmed a secret suspicion, somehow publicly justified, that
there is a strong streak of arrogance running through the
national character.

Arrogance, you may call it. Or confidence, if you are of a
gentler and more forgiving disposition. Why has this city for
so long been such a temple of high fashion? It is only in recent
years, and well within living memory, that the English and
the Italians have produced, nurtured even, names that stand
in clear rivalry to Dior and St Laurent. Most of those whose
job it is, or whose purse and taste will allow, have now heard
of Giorgio Armani in Milan and Bruce Oldfield in London.
But for a long post-war time, if it wasn't French, it wasn't
fashionable.

The appearance of the city justifies this theory of arrogance. In the euphoria of the Napoleonic victories, Monsieur
Haussmann was commissioned to clear away large parts of
the old city, to create a star, L'Étoile, in a prominent and visible position; and to forge his boulevards which, from that
central point, would lead you from the Arch triumphantly
out, or collect you, from a less privileged district, and guide
you, triumphantly, in. There were, even in those early days,
small cries of disaffection from those who wished to see the
medieval parts of the city restored and preserved. But the
grand design was executed with speed, and, when you stand
on the top of the Arc de Triomphe, you would be rightly
accused of churlishness if you didn't admit that the concept
works majestically. The world's biggest flag, a Tricolore,
flaps and wafts under the Arch. Perfectly in proportion, and
irritatingly proportional.

Look at the Eiffel Tower. It is infinitely less graceful than
Blackpool Tower, and as a central landmark, or a point of
identification, it cannot be seen from many parts of the city.
And yet it has been absorbed into the tradition of the place.
Eiffel, when he had designed it, said he wanted no half
measures. The conservative and voluble citizens of Paris said
it was dreadful, and, if it had to be there, couldn't someone
afford to finish it. Eiffel, in indignant mood, said or pretended (which is better) that he had no idea what they meant.
They meant that they had no wish to see naked steel girders

topped by a small crown. Why couldn't he box it in, make it look more like a finished Cleopatra's Needle, that sort of thing? That's how it was designed, responded M. Eiffel, and that's how it will stay.

If we are bent upon the differences between them, the French, and us (the English), how better to illustrate the enormous divide of La Manche than in this determined attitude to building. Do you remember when plans for the extension to the National Gallery, in Trafalgar Square in London, were laid before the governors? There were odd little murmurs of disapproval. But nothing was said until Prince Charles complained loudly and publicly about a 'carbuncle'. The plans were instantly shelved, and a new competition ordained.

Pompidou wouldn't have shilly-shallied. An eminent British architect, Richard Rogers, helped to design the Centre Pompidou, the cultural complex otherwise known as the Beaubourg. An enormous explosion rocked the city of Paris. Ugly, they said. An excrescence. Out of keeping. A factory.

'Build it!' said M. Pompidou. Was he confident about its eventual success? Was he arrogant? Or was he just French? Or, heaven help us, in this dissection of the Parisian psyche, was he an energetic combination of all these things?

All that need be said at this stage is that however distressing this building may appear to a traditionalist, it is extremely popular. Visitors enjoy themselves joy-riding up and down the escalators and elevators which are clamped to the outside of the structure. If you squinnied your eyes and adopted a narrower perspective, you could imagine yourself inside the boiler room of some great liner. It is colourful too, and the great concourse or parterre outside is widely patronised by the world's youth . . . performing, applauding, swallowing fire, selling beads, showing off their dogs, conjuring rats from hats (and vice versa), arguing about the architectural merits of the Centre Pompidou. Those responsible for such dubious statistics say, with conviction, confidence or arrogance, that this place entertains more visitors daily than the traditional sights of the Louvre or Notre Dame. M. Pompidou avait raison.

I left the British Embassy late in the afternoon with Lady Fretwell. She wanted to show me one of her favourite private spots in Paris. We drove with some speed and style in an Embassy car past the front of the Louvre, where there are gigantic roadworks. The whole courtyard which faces the bottom of the Champs Elysées is being excavated and a strange, shining, space-like pyramid being lowered into the historic earth. In the bold tradition of Haussmann, Eiffel, Rogers and Pompidou, here is the latest public manifestation of the Parisian determination to make a mark on the land-scape. This front pyramid, which will serve as a grand entrance to one of the world's gloomier buildings, is being engineered at the express presidential command.

Eventually, we arrived in the outer fringes of the Bois de Boulogne. The driver was ordered to proceed at a slower speed, but not so slow as to be illegal. Here, on either side of the road, some in full blousy blatancy, and others under the candles of a blooming chestnut, were groups of Brazilian transvestites. This is their particular patch. They lounge and tout for passing motor trade. We kept moving, until we took a small détour to arrive at the Shakespeare Garden. Here, almost every day, comes a bubbly and enthusiastic French-woman, Marie-Louise Hemphill, who has helped to carve out a little open-air theatre in the Bois. It is a private garden, supported by charity, and making a little money for itself by using the stage for various recitals and performances. Every plant or flower which Shakespeare mentions in the plays, the sonnets and the poems, grows, at some time of the year, in this pleasing bosky confusion.

I said goodbye to Lady Fretwell and handed her a sprig of rosemary. That, as Ophelia distractedly observed, is for remembrance.

'I shall drive you back to Paris,' said Marie-Louise Hemp-hill. I thanked her, wandered pleasurably round the warm, sweet-smelling garden, and then got into her little car, one with a stick gear jutting from the dashboard, for the return journey to the city. It will be a long time before I forget this drive. She is a charming companion but seems unaware that other cars are legally entitled to use the public roads. It would be discourteous of me to write the words that escaped from my anguished lips in the course of this career into the city. We swept through traffic lights and mounted the pavement wherever there seemed no immediate right of way. Innocent pedestrians going about the business of the streets suddenly started to behave like hysterical chickens, caught in the middle of pecking their farmyard corn, by a demented tractor. All this was conducted by one hand. The other she used for unwrapping a variety of chocolates. When, eventually, I persuaded her to put me down, she said I looked pale and shouldn't we go to a café or a bar for a little restoratif. There are other memorable journeys to share on this Grand Tour, but the drivers used both hands.

★   ★   ★

Le style français has, I am sure, something to do with being lazy. This is the voice of the Northern Protestant calling. The Metro runs on rubber wheels so that a decent matutinal reverie is not shaken into reality. The French were the first people to put Coke and lemonade and soda water into small squirting things like baby petrol pumps, so that, presumably, they didn't need to waste any energy levering off a tight cap. Le Self-Service, though basically of American origin, was adopted and refined in Europe by the French. Am I being unfair? Well, if you think so, remind yourself of that supremely simple invention used by the 'chiffoniers' in the parks. 'Why,' said a tired and backaching picker-up of fallen leaves, 'why must I spend every day bending down to pick up a shovel full of nature's autumnal droppings?' And his neighbour, similarly doubled and troubled, said, 'If we knocked a sharp point into a stick, we could walk, talk, stroll even, through the park, and pick up our leaves, and never have to bend our tired backs again.' Is that invention mothered by necessity? No. Is it inspired by laziness? Maybe.

These animadversions were running through my mind when I saw my first Parisian motorised pooper-scooper. Part of the city's grand contemporary design is to make the streets clean again. And a part of the daily ritual of any self-respecting Frenchwoman, of the middle years, is to take her dog for a breath of fresh air, along the boulevards, into the square, and back home for a gentle aperitif and a gossip about the day's affairs. She always takes the same route, and the dog has long since staked its territorial claims at this street corner, and on the far side of that tree. The dog seems elegantly laundered, shampooed and set. Which is why there is always a distressing moment when the wretched thing will behave as though it is an animal. La Française is used to all this. She has long practice of gazing into a shop window, or suddenly finding it necessary to search for something in her handbag, whilst the dog squats inelegantly and seems to have little or no shame.

Well, the civic authorities of Paris are having no more of that, merci beaucoup. No sooner has the evacuated dog scraped the imaginary earth, never having got to evolutionary grips with the difference between pavements and lawns, than out of the mists, like Peter Fonda in an early biking movie, rides a motorcyclist, goggled, helmeted, fully motorised, driving what appears to be a large double-tubed vacuum cleaner. He puts out one leather-clad foot to steady

Trottoirs Nets! Keep Paris Tidy.

his angry machine and turns on a switch. There is a swoosh-ing sound. He manoeuvres the nozzle exactly over the offen-sive deposit. Something happens. One is initially too embar-rassed to make too close an inspection. There is more swooshing. The biker plays a macho tune on his throttle. Something like a hairdryer then pokes its bristly head from the tube. There is even more swooshing. Then a humming silence . . . a roar . . . and the bike and driver screech away, leaving the pavement clean, dry, pristine. If only, I think, that every brick one has dropped, every mess one has made, on that awkward travel between the cradle and the grave, could be cleared away so efficiently. And yet, stroking the philosophical stem of another glass of wine, would one really wish to live one's life in the confines of a clinic?

★   ★   ★

Time to leave this not altogether sympathetic capital. Bos-well, in earlier times, was told that the only sensible way to travel was to bring his own carriage from England. He would, thereby, avoid some of the discomforts and expense of foreign hire. If he couldn't do it this way, he would have to make local application for a diligence, a 'coche' or a 'carasse', with the consequent bother about horses, their feeding, watering and stabling, and the strong possibility of a grum-bling and greedy groom, running away and wanting his liquor and women, as Mr Eliot would have put it.

They say things are easier now. A taxi whisks me from the hotel to the Gare de Lyon. I use the journey to speculate again upon the nature of the stranger who is conducting me. At one traffic light, to test the water, as it were, I tapped him on the shoulder and said, 'Thank you for helping me at this stage of the Grand Tour.'

You could see that he was beginning to fear he had a mad-man as a passenger. His eyes narrowed and he made a noise like 'Mmmm.' Thereafter, he made the taxi go more quickly and there were few politenesses exchanged at the early morning terminal.

He made no effort to help me with my bags, which began to assume some independent life, like falling over. I left the collection of cases on the pavement to go to search for a trolley. The wealthier of our original travellers would have had their bags collected, taken to the coach and stowed. It would have been unlikely one of them would have contained a bomb. Here, at the Gare de Lyon, the trolleys were stacked at the far end of the building, and locked into each other in the manner of a Sainsbury's entrance hall.

Somebody, the enterprising Frenchman, is making a fortune out of this system. You have to push a ten-franc piece into a box attached to the handle of the trolley. This releases the mechanism which allows you to push the pram away. These gadgets, which were designed to assist the flustered traveller, seem to develop a mind of their own, once they are running free. The wheels suddenly skewer off at a random tangent, and the trolley crashes into the unprotected heels of an angry fellow traveller. There is little effort made to explain to the hirer how he claims back his ten francs. The train is due to pull away in two minutes and someone is clearly trading in the commerce of panic. Leave it! It's only ten francs. If four thousand disadvantaged tourists behave like this every day, somebody, somewhere, is smiling at the precise conquest of a moving market.

One suspected weakness in my psychological make-up has been regularly confirmed by this Grand Tour. I am not prepared to leave much to chance. I must arrive at the train, the boat, the 'plane at least half an hour before the required time. I am now constitutionally incapable of dicing with time. It is a naked display of the 'What if?' syndrome. What if there's a traffic jam? What if there's a puncture? What if the security check takes much longer? What if the 'thing' I am travelling in, or by, actually leaves on time? Never, you note, 'what if it doesn't?'

At the Gare de Lyon, I had to use a large computer to get a boarding ticket. First class, one way, Paris-Lyon. It sounds easy. It was, yet again, an autocratic challenge. Tedium, and to be honest, an almost complete lack of understanding, prevents me from rehearsing the micro-chipped options opened to me by the ticket dispenser. I could not find an old-fashioned guichet, with a prim bespectacled single lady, who would take time and care to make sure that I had the right document. That's what I wanted. Instead, there were a lot of flashing lights, and ribbons of printed-out requests, each posing a series of urgent alternatives. Suppose the time runs out on Question 7a and you have to start at the top again, with all these impatient French computer whizz-kids in the queue behind you, tapping their heels, sighing, looking at their watches, and exchanging sympathetic glances with each other . . . The sympathy, of course, is for themselves. None for me.

There is an odd philanthropic conclusion to the story of my early departure for Lyon. So used had I become to the freeing and retrieving of the trolleys, so computer-friendly with the ticket machine, after so much Parisian to-ing and fro-ing, that I found time and a reservoir of good will with which to help the less fortunate. And these included a lot of French travellers, who were not too thrilled to be assisted to play their own machines by a wandering Angle.

The train ticket tells you exactly where to sit. Carriage number. Window seat. Facing engine. Smoking. No room for doubt. No possibility of a mistake. The TGV leaves on time. It is a point of honour, if not of principle, I suspect that the guard on the platform, telepathically tuned into the driver, would wait for no man. Not the British Ambassador, not the Mayor of Paris, not Rudolf Nureyev or Charlotte Rampling. Probably not even for those little anonymous men and women whom M. le Directeur at Michelin dispatches out to the four corners of Europe, clutching last year's little red book, with their mission to spread the gastronomic gospel. And certainly not for me.

We slid out of the Gare de Lyon at ten of the clock. A digital clock, at that. Two and a bit hours of 'grande vitesse' to the city that thinks it should be the capital, from the city that knows it is.

CHAPTER
TWO

The 'banlieues', the suburbs of Paris look very much like any domestically huddled Betjeman fringe. There are games to be played even on this seemingly ordinary stretch of the tour. If you think back to the Deux Magots and the voluptuous or suicidal possibility of every seventh person, you can throw the dice of chance by changing people for houses. Some people think that houses can be warmer and more comfortable than close encounters of the seventh kind.

The TGV may get you there, and on time, but it does not live up to the excitements of its simple and rapid title. I had expected food and wine of the highest order. I had, after all, once travelled to Paris on the Golden Arrow, with white napkins in starched folds, with an aperitif, drunk legally under age, with rattling silver, and a steaming dish of chicken, with sparkling glasses of a proper vintage, and the waft of a successful businessman's fat cigar. There's none of that here. Rather disappointingly, you are served with a plastic tray of short-haul foods, like the stuff you refuse on an aeroplane. Convenience, I believe it's called. But whose?

Ploughing south from Paris, and soon you find yourself in an open, cultivated landscape. Little there is that pricks the nerve of excitement. There is no mystery in a ploughed field.

So I put my half-picked tray to one side, to consider my progress so far.

★   ★   ★

I commenced my Grand Tour in the most inauspicious of circumstances. Months before the date of departure I had booked myself aboard a Townsend-Thoresen ferry from Dover to Ostend. Why Ostend? Two reasons. Firstly, I had never been there before, and secondly, it was handy: I had planned to travel to Bruges, Brussels, to look at the Battlefield of Waterloo, and thence, south to Paris.

A week before I left Dover, I was listening to the news on Radio 4, and heard of the ferry, Spirit of Free Enterprise, keeling over in Zeebrugge harbour. No need to rehearse the awful details of this capsize, except to say that it has, sadly, become one of those significant dates in the diary of disasters whereby you mark a personal movement. Aberfan, Kennedy's assassination, and, more recently, Enniskillen, King's Cross and Zeebrugge. Before the catastrophe, it seemed that the safest way to cross that part of the Channel was by ferry, and Townsend-Thoresen at that. Everyone was wiser and more careful after the event. The sea was calm, the sun shone, and, were it not for the horror of the previous week, one would have been in a mood of anticipatory enjoyment.

Except, and there are always these nagging exceptions, except that two events on the open sea served to remind me that though I might have the trappings and services and the serious intentions of the Grand Tourist, I was still at the mercy of chance. By nature, I am as careful as can be in the planning of a journey. I am still surprised and annoyed when these well-laid plans are thwarted. I had decided to cast off in some style, to which end I had ordered a picnic hamper from 'Mr Pie-Man', a local London shop which supplies good foods, even though you have seriously to think about a second mortgage if you are planning anything ambitious. When I say hamper, I do not mean that sweating porters had to heave a heavy whicker basket up a gang plank. I mean something portable and discreet.

The hamper contained smoked salmon sandwiches, quails' eggs and a bottle of Chablis. I looked for a quiet corner on an upper deck, smelled the fresh North Sea air, settled down with a newspaper, and found myself confronted by a rowdy bunch of fellow travellers. They were in high good humour. They were a group of boisterous dentists (collective noun not known) and they were off to Ostend for a stag weekend. The prospective groom was accompanied by his father. There were plenty of jokes about dentures and the sowing of dragon's teeth, and there were also big plastic carrier bags full of tins of lager which had to be emptied before we docked.

So far, I had imagined that I could remain comfortably anonymous behind sunglasses and newspaper. But they were on the hunt and looking for a 'bit of fun'.

The line of immediate defence is to punch them with questions.

'Who's the lucky woman?'

'Plucky woman you mean. Ha ha!' General amusement.

'When's the wedding, then?' I ask, as if interested.

'Well, it'd better be bloody quick or t'baby'll be there as well! Ha ha!' More roars.

'He's brought his Dad with 'im in case he needs his nappy changing!'

'Ha ha,' I laugh in a weak way.

'Fancy a lager then, lad?'

'Give him one of your egg butties,' commands another. 'He needs fattening up!'

I do not now see any immediate way out of this impromptu but relentless party which is forming round me. A well-developed sense of self-preservation persuades me that I should keep the lowest possible profile.

'Where are you going then, Russell?'

Why is it that I cannot bring myself to say that this is the first hour of the first day of my Grand Tour of Europe? Why cannot I take the initiative and tell them about Boswell and Smollett and make them understand that, in some way, I am trying to be as venturesome as Lady Mary Wortley Montagu, who, because of the rough seas off Calais, jumped in her parachute skirts from the main deck of her ship into the rowing boat which would take her safely into the harbour.

'Where are you going then, Russell?'

I'm going a-milking, sir, she said, and then tried to make the explanation as brief and as unattractive as possible. It didn't really work.

'All right for bloody some people, isn't it! Pity this poor bugger who's got to get hitched next weekend, while you're swanning off. Look at his Dad. Pity *he* didn't! Ha ha! Give our Russell another lager.'

This was clearly not the moment to offer them a glass of lightly chilled Chablis. The ship ploughed on. The dentists cracked open yet more tins of lager. The conversation became more raucous. We slithered into Ostend, and as the great ship turned into the harbour, I discovered that I had been burned by a lethal combination of sea-wind and sun. Since I was a child I have been badly burned by any direct exposure to sunlight. It happens quickly and the consequences are unpleasant. My hands swell and my face explodes and I become tetchy and depressed and irritated and miserable. I've taken every pill, and used every ointment, and all to no effect.

I left the boat in poor shape, with an unread copy of my newspaper, and the ludicrous prospect of having to declare at the Customs shed the useless importation of one bottle of by now decently warmed Chablis, and half a dozen lightly boiled quails' eggs.

Not the most romantic of starts.

I will not waste my time or yours by inventing some grand and glorious entry into the strange lands of 'abroad'. Ostend, sadly, is to me worth only the forgetting. The first night I lay in bed with two wet towels wrapped around two hot pieces of roast pork, formerly my hands, and listened to BBC Radio 4, and wished I'd been sensible and stayed at home.

By the time I reached the city of Bruges, God had turned down the sun's regulo, and I felt a little more cheerful. This was my first visit. I had read enough about it. It is a convenient city for travel editors of weekend newspapers. The centre is full of charming houses which fit neatly into composed pictures. There are languid and contained canals. Northern canals, that is. Staid and rather formal waterways which go nowhere, and have never experienced the wash of an urgent vaporetto. In the streets, whatever is not a chocolate shop is a lace shop. I can see that God was enjoying him-self when he stumbled upon the idea of chocolate. I am not able to read the divine mind upon the subject of lace. I fear that lace-makers approach their delicate task with the same relentless energy, the same singularity of an almost pointless purpose, as those who dedicate themselves to building models of the Forth Bridge out of mis-spent matches. There must be a point to it. It's just that I can't see it.

The rage of my wretched sunburn began to abate when I arrived at the hotel. And this is as convenient a moment as any to explain how an hotel can have a dramatic effect upon my attitude to a place. I have stayed of necessity in many, many hotels, and I can sort them into my own categories very speedily; the size of a place, or other people's arbitrary rating, doesn't matter to me. I have the sense of a smoke detector, a geiger counter. I walked into the Swan Hotel, Die Swaene, in Bruges, and felt better, less stressed, not yet relaxed, but with all the possibility of it.

I hadn't by any means shuffled off my English concerns. I was not yet a tourist facing South. I had half an eye cocked towards home.

'Can I get Radio 4?'

'Yezsir,'

'Can I get BBC 2?'

'Yezsir.'

'Can I have a drink?'

'Yezsir.'

Bags were transported swiftly to a charming large room on the ground floor. The windows opened on to a small courtyard. There was no sound except for the evening bells. Radio 4 and BBC 2, both loud and clear, and a firm promise of *The Times* tomorrow morning.

I have long campaigned for hotel managers to spend the whole of one night in each of their beds. Then they would know what joy a restful night brings, and how the switch of the bed-light, just out of reach, can turn the next day into a cloudy and depressing encounter.

The Swan has every switch right. The Swan also has an untemperamental and efficient shower. I need to write a handbook to the showers of Europe. They can have a fearful life of their own if you don't watch them. Turn your back, and they become vicious and writhing snakes, possessed of a desire and powered by an energy to destroy you. There are so many variations. So many modern applications which disguise the difference between 'hot' and 'cold'. So many connected, in some obscure way, to the bath taps. Some freeze you with an embarrassing trickle. Others flatten you against the far wall, and at that moment, you realise you need ankle irons to keep you vertical. To mention nothing of the bathroom floor which becomes a towel-soaked swamp.

Bruges in the early summer evening has all the right enchantments, in domestic proportion. The coachloads have gone to an early dinner at their Novotels, and there is little civic bustle. The chocolatiers are about their sweet-smelling business, and the lace-makers, behind large wooden warehouse doors, silently weave another delicate web, and the one on the left never stops her vital fingers to enquire, from the one on the right, exactly why they imitate the action of a spider. Walking home to The Swan for a nightcap, I have made a traveller's note that I must go to the Groeninge Museum tomorrow. It will become clearer to you that, on this Grand Tour, I am not powered by the highest artistic motives. I am not travelling in order to see the *Mona Lisa*. If and when I get there, I shall not spend an hour in a queue at the Uffizi in Florence, nor take sandwiches to the Parthenon. Coals are best left in Newcastle.

But I have a suspicious smell about the Groeninge. Outside it seems insignificant. There is a small sign, like that of a humble shopkeeper, making almost a shy announcement of its presence.

After a restful night, with my hands assuming a more Dürer-like grace; after a tall glass of fresh orange juice, with bits of fruit clinging still to the sides, bits which you would lick out if you weren't well behaved, and do, whether or not; after thick, freshly toasted brown bread and home-made marmalade; and after a hesitant tap on the door asking if you would like a fresh pot of coffee; then you are of a mood to walk the newly aired streets and look at the Flemish pictures in this handsome museum.

Pictures as furniture. That was the second lesson I ever

learned at Oxford. I was taught for three expandingly happy years by Professor Nevill Coghill. He was riding a popular cloud, with his newly published translation of Chaucer's *Canterbury Tales*, and when I walked into his suite of rooms in Exeter College, I could sense that this was something new to me, but something I would naturally wish to emulate. Books as furniture was the first lesson. At home, in Blackburn, I had to be secretive about books. They were not encouraged. Why should I want to use the Public Library? Library books were a natural harbour for various diseases. Mrs Lucas swore that her daughter, Doreen, caught diphtheria from her library book. All I can say, at this stage, is that Doreen got off very lightly if that was all she caught. Why, in God's name, am I thinking of Doreen Lucas in the entrance hall of the Groeninge? She is not the *seventh* person to pass through this morning's turnstile – is she?

Pictures as furniture is the theme, and Coghill was its author. And everywhere I have since lived, I have made into a personal nest, and lined the walls with books and with pictures. The Groeninge is an utterly charming and easily manageable gallery. You can see everything in and on its small walls and halls within the space of half a relaxed hour. If you turn left as you go through the modest front door, you start with the early Flemish masters. They are consumed with the superstition and primitive power of God, Jesus, the crucifixion, hell, damnation, punishment and paradise. Their patron was the powerfully rich Medieval Church, and in order to explain stories from the Bible, to fortify the faithful and terrify the faithless, there on the walls are vivid examples of what you could expect. And paintings such as Gerard David's *The Judgement of Cambyses* demonstrate how the secular masters picked up the same kind of habits from their religious masters.

Then the city became a busy centre for rich weavers. Nothing in man's nature has changed radically in the last half-millennium. If you've got it, flaunt it. Today, with a modest degree of self-recognition, you could hire the services of Hockney or Bryan Organ, to paint you in your successful landscape. The rich burghers had themselves recorded at the height of their commercial and social prosperity. There seems little attempt to flatter. You paid for what you got, and you got what you were. As interesting as the round cheese faces of the Master and his wife are the black and white uncluttered interiors. A pet bird, a pampered dog, a wayward child, carefully arranged at the edges of their lives.

Whoever heard of a bowl of fruit being the subject of a painting? The young apprentice artist probably complained. No, the Master of the house replied, stroking his purse. My wife has a bowl of fruit and she likes her bowl of fruit and that's what I want in my picture.

They were the new patrons.

In the natural progress of history, which this gallery unfolds, you arrive at a moment of imperialism. Time to look abroad, and fight for territory. Time to extend the bounds of influence. Time for conquest. Here the canvases expand to accommodate mighty sea battles, clouds of gun-smoke, vast loops of sail, the rumour, then the noise, almost the smell, of war.

In this gallery, the distinct periods of development are no more than suggested. You are not overwhelmed. You are not preached at pictorially, nor taught any kind of chauvinistic lesson. All is in domestic harmony, even when you come face to face with the twentieth century.

In the corner of this room, near to the end of your rect-angular perambulation, there is a girl, sitting on the floor, her hands clasped around her knees, with her head fallen for-ward, almost in sleep. She seems to have drifted away, in a private reverie. Should she be disturbed? Will the attendant ask her to get up and move on? The reason why she isn't breathing is that she is cast in bronze, and left there to cause the browser a moment's disquiet. Until, that is, you hear the twittering of a bird. Above the sleeping girl, and part of the dotty modern collection, is a large picture, cunningly three-dimensional, with windows that are mirrors, and a painted bird cage which contains a live finch. A finch in the Groen-inge. It produces the same strange thrill as a swear word in a church.

There is no family picture of the owners of The Swan Hotel. And that's a pity. They would make an interesting composition. It wasn't until I was preparing to leave this haven that I realised what was going on. There was an ever-present young man at the desk. Dark, small moustache, nothing too much trouble. I might order a gin and tonic from him. I like this served in the room with a flourish and a smile, and not the impersonal concoctions of a soulless mini-bar. And before I would arrive in my room myself, he was there serving it. As I passed through the hall on my way out, I would express my admiration at the young man's speedy service. He would look back at me, slightly puzzled. It was not until the identical young twins arrived to take my bags that I realised I had been deceived by my own eyes. Here was a *Comedy of Errors*. Antipholus of Ephesus brought the drinks. Antipholus of Syracuse was in charge of the desk. To make ostentatious amends, I was forced to double the tip. They didn't mind. Neither, for that matter, in this comfortable rest house, did I.

Brussels is now a power house of deliberation, politicking energy, hi-technology, diplomacy, bureaucracy, more or less anything that ends in 'acy', and costs millions of pounds, marks, francs per second; and yet it appears to have made no significant ripple on the map of European history. It reminds me of the story one rather famous English actress tells about herself. She was, she says, sitting in a railway carriage (as, indeed, I am now). A child opposite stared at her for quite a time and then turned to the accompanying mother and said, 'What's that lady for?'

I doubt if Brussels knows the answer. It sounds harsh, I know, but it's an attitude which has gradually crystallised. 'Wait till you see the Grand Place!' they say, trying to persuade me of some positive virtue. 'It's beautiful.' It is. But it's a sort of theatrical history set. There's little behind it. You half expect, when you wander behind the Town Hall, to see all the delicate fretwork of a Hollywood set. The Place is also over-guarded. Police materialise from every corner, glare and stare, move you on, swing their threatening batons, or finger their holsters in a threatening manner.

'Wait till you have had one of Brussels' delicious meals.'

Brussels, they say, is one of the gastronomic posthouses of the continent. It also happens to be the one place on the whole of the Grand Tour that delivered the food onto my lap instead of my plate. Perhaps there was an earth tremor. Perhaps the waiter had a 'crise de nerfs'. I don't know. There was precious little attempt at an apology. Maybe I was thinking rather too grandly for a tourist. I half expected my jacket to be spirited away to an all-night cleaners. At least the manager, whom I caught in half-smirk at my misfortune, could have presented his card and offered to pay the cleaning bill. I don't think this red-plush overpriced slap-happy café would have been placed into the hands of the receivers if they had suggested a marginal reduction when the bill was presented. That didn't disappear under the table. It was pinned firmly to the plate. This place doesn't appear in the Red Michelin Guide. I am not surprised.

There was none of this nonsense at the EEC Headquarters at Berleymont – a ghastly modern building plonked in the middle of the city. If this place had been designed to avoid any reference to a home, a character, a personal reminder, a holiday shop even, then it succeeds admirably. You could be anywhere. You could be nowhere. If it hadn't been for an appointment with the red-haired, no-nonsense Barbara Castle, I wouldn't have stayed another pre-stressed concrete minute.

I have known Mrs Castle for a long time. She was the family MP in Blackburn, and my parents, staunch unquestioning Tories, secretly voted for Barbara Castle, but not, oh dear me, *not* for the Labour Party. Somehow, it didn't seem to matter that Mrs Castle was a member of the Labour Party. As long as it was she who represented the Borough's interests at the Palace of Westminster, they were happy. And this cult of the personal vote didn't worry Barbara, who rode from Blackburn to Westminster on a powerful popular vote.

In those days, of course, an MP was as grand and remote a figure as the Mayor. You would stand when one or the other, or both, entered the room. They were the pre-soap pop stars. When my best friend's mother became the Mayor of Blackburn, and my friend became, by ties of nature, the Mayoress, I became happily involved in the business of civic display. The Mayor was Edith Railton. Her daughter,

Madge (now Hindle), the Mayoress. They spent a glittering year in their robes and chains. They turned many a stuffy occasion into a party, and they had, perforce, to work closely with our Member, Mrs Castle. The same Mrs Castle, now a Euro-member in a blank office, the same Mrs Castle waiting to take me on a tour of this democratic turbine, the same member who would eventually lead me to the Council Chambers of Europe.

It was during the Mayoralty of Edith Railton that the Blackburn Agricultural Show was instituted. At one point, on the opening day, when Mayoress Madge and an important party from the Council were sitting in a kind of medieval pavilion, the Mayor and the MP went on an official tour of the arena. They were both wearing unsuitable clothes . . . high heels, posh stockings, hats, handbags. It had rained for three days. The arena was a large and treacherous bog, churned by wellingtons, animal hooves and tractor tyres. The loud speaker system was operated by one of those gentlemen inordinately satisfied by the echo of his own voice. There was no breathing space in the commentary. At precisely that moment, when the Mayor and Mrs Castle turned to visit another class, the announcer proclaimed, 'Ladies and Gentlemen, the fat cattle are now entering the ring!' There was an enormous gale of laughter and a cheer for these two intrepid trudgers. They joined in the fun, but neither of them won prizes. When they came back to the tent, however, people examined their rosettes with some scepticism.

I reminded my host of this historic occasion. We were standing in a queue in the cafeteria at the EEC. It had been made plain that there would be no nonsense about a restaurant, waiter service, napkins, all that lot. 'That's for the big nobs,' she said. 'We'll manage in the ordinary canteen.'

When I had made my first call to Barbara, to try to arrange this meeting, she said she was going to be very busy, and when would I be there? 'I'm thinking I'll be there Friday night,' I said, with half an eye on the diary. 'And, perhaps, we could meet on Saturday, say at lunch time?' There was a pause, with a sigh in it.

'Have you ever been to Brussels?' she enquired.

'No I haven't which is why I am wanting to see you.'

'Well, clearly you haven't. There is no such thing as a weekend. It closes on Friday afternoons. The airport is jammed. Why don't you come to Hell Fire Corner, where I live in England, and I'll cook you something.'

'The point is, I am a Grand Tourer, passing through Brussels, hoping to meet those who live and work there. You, for example.'

'I'll be out of it, darling. Fast as my little legs will get me.'

She is extraordinarily well regarded at the EEC. When she walks down a corridor, or approaches the bar (a hot bed of democratic mixing), you can see people whispering to each other that Mrs Castle is amongst them. She is a small, smart woman. Her presence comes not from height or heavy weight, but from an almost burning fierceness. She is, also, handsome, perhaps a little vain. It does her absolutely no harm. Her profile, in this unattractive jungle, is high.

When we got to the check-out desk in the cafeteria, she shouted back down the line, where I was still dithering over the choice of cheesecakes, 'We're going Dutch on this. I can't afford to be paying for you.'

'Leave it, Barbara,' I shouted back. 'I'll do it all.'

'No you won't. You'll be telling people you bribed me.' We had a splendid gossip at table. People came to join us for a paragraph. Then excused themselves. Somebody she doesn't exactly love is Lord Jim Callaghan. Somebody she doesn't exactly hate is Margaret Thatcher.

'You get the coffee. You're younger than most of them round here.' I'm not, but I do. And when this snack was finished, I stood to escort her out.

'Listen, lad, you have to take your tray and all your dirty pots to that dispenser thing over there. There's nobody here to clear up for you. What they call the democratic principle. Pick that serviette up.'

She went off to prepare herself for the afternoon's committee meetings. She arranged for me to sit at the back of this particular chamber. The arena is rather like a smaller version of the United Nations Assembly. Almost everybody wears headphones for the simultaneous translations. I wasn't able to follow the main thrust of the deliberations, and I am not sure that anyone else could.

When I'd had enough, I crept down the side aisle, just as the voting had started. I turned at the big spring doors to wave farewell, and to mouth 'Thanks.' She waved back, but I fear that her vigorous semaphore was taken for a negative vote in the Steel Production Quota. And as everyone knows, Barbara is always so positive.

No wonder the EEC works the way it does!

★   ★   ★

I am beginning to feel like a baton, passed by one panting runner to another, as in some hectic Olympic relay. Dropped, occasionally, seized with great vigour, and carried with speed to some new exchange. This thought occurs to me as I sit staring out of the Train de Grande Vitesse. Hurtling through the middle of France and heading southwards to the City of Lyon. Me and several hungry rats of reporters smelling the stinking story of Klaus Barbie who is to face trial in the city, for crimes against humanity committed during the Nazi rule of Germany. That is another cruel avenue I have not yet explored. At this time, and at 160 m.p.h., in an armchair with my back to the engine, I am in a mood of tranquillity recollected in motion.

★   ★   ★

I arrived in the little town of Waterloo with the present Marquis of Anglesey. We were looking for his great-great grandfather's leg which was shot off at the height of the battle. The Earl of Uxbridge was sitting on his horse, surveying the battle as it approached its climax.

'By God, Uxbridge,' Wellington barked. 'You've lost your leg.'

And being the almost perfect one-legged Englishman, he put the glorious resolution of this present encounter with the enemy higher in his list of priorities than any such personal trifle as the loss of an appendage. When he could snatch a moment, he looked down at himself.

'By God, sir, so I have!'

The Marquis of Anglesey retains vestiges of the Uxbridge

phlegm. We made little progress in finding the glorified dog kennel which now houses Uxbridge's hapless limb.

'Oh, for God's sake, it's round here somewhere,' he said, mopping his brow with an upper-class English handkerchief which looked like half of the Red Ensign.

'Why don't we go into a café or one of those things. What do you call them . . . er . . . bars! A bar is what we want. They'll tell us.'

I wonder whether, in what schoolboys call 'the olden days', the uncertain travellers felt the same urge to seek comfort in alcohol. I do not want to suggest that this journey was accomplished on a comfortable cushion of alcohol, but it would be deceitful to deny the help that you get from a little social oiling.

'Nous chercherons la jambe de l'Earl d'Uxbridge,' declared Anglesey in sonorous tones. 'Mais, d'abord, deux verres de votre Guinness, s'il vous plait.'

I'm glad he had the nerve to ask. Consider the pitfalls and potholes in the construction and pronunciation of that complicated question. Is it de l'Earl? Is it d'Uxbridge? 'De' sounds preposterous when it is bolted up against Uxbridge. There are also several 'u' sounds which always trap me in any effort to pronounce standard English and, especially so, when I am in the company of a Marquis.

We were given directions, and once the froth was off the Guinness, we set out on this bizarre little pilgrimage. Waterloo looks like a side street in Uxbridge. There are chemists and paper shops, fruit stalls and frock shops. It's busy of a mid-morning. One earnest Frenchman, having intelligence of our quest, took us finally to a most un-prepossessing resting ground. Rusty iron gates. An overgrown yard in front of a house that looked as though it had recently been abandoned by a busted commune, a heavily bloomed lilac bush bursting out of a bed of tell-tale nettles. Tin cans, a tyre, and enough dog dirt to keep a novice Parisian scooper in business for half a day.

And there, with little trails of ivy and a pot with an odd flower, was the tomb. Here is no Pharoah's outlasting monument; none of Napoleon's almost arrogant porphyry as displayed in the Invalides. In some ways it's a little like a doll's house. A dotty relic of a bloody battle. Quite touching.

The field of Waterloo has been reorganised. The Marquis of Anglesey reckons that neither Wellington nor Napoleon would recognise it. It's a mile or two outside the town. The topography is open and undulating. But when you turn off the main road, to follow the signpost for the exact spot, you are suddenly confronted by a large pyramid, built of earth, covered with grass and crowned by a plinth upon which stands an angry proud lion, cast in iron, staring at a now silent landscape.

At one corner of this monument is a narrow staircase which leads you from the field to the summit. As we rose to survey the scene, the Marquis reminded me that we were to have a view of this cockpit which no general, no leader or soldier could have seen. When the turbulent affairs of battle

La Jambe de l'Earl d'Uxbridge

had been settled by the diplomats, there descended upon Waterloo all kinds of visitors ravenous for the pickings of a great military victory. The French Revolution and the Napoleonic Wars brought a sudden halt to the fashionable run of the Grand Tour. You could never tell, then, when the border of a country had been re-drawn, or even, at any given moment, who was the victor and who had disappeared to disgraceful exile. Here, around these cornfields and pastures, there arrived coach loads of the four-wheeled variety. They were looking for bullets, for buttons and batons. The wilier of the locals opened little stalls to sell quick polled accounts of the day's sweeping activities. Cannon balls were a popular buy. Some chipped out stones from the farmhouses at La Sainte Haye and Huguémont because they bore the round holes of fiery battle.

George IV went to see for himself and took the Duke of Wellington with him. They hoped that they might find the Earl of Uxbridge's then-missing leg, but they met Lord Byron instead. He was there for the still-lingering smell of action and, rather unwisely, he said to the Royal party that he was 'damned sorry' that Napoleon had been defeated. That, as you might expect, was neither a popular nor a tactful remark.

You would not, today, find out much about the victorious Iron Duke. The souvenir shops, the cafés and the odd bar concentrate all their commercial energy on Bonaparte. The laurels of the Emperor decorate doors and walls and windows. France, after all, isn't that far away.

When the Marquis of Anglesey and I reached the top of the monument in a breathless state, it began to thunder and to rain. The morning, strangely, had been calm. Indeed, back in the town of Waterloo, we sat for half an hour on a bench, in the sunshine, talking of this and that. But suddenly, as though to provide a suitable accompaniment to the field's fury, the wind whipped out of the West, and we had difficulty shouting and listening to each other.

On 18 June 1815, the morning of the battle, the fields were sodden. The corn and grass were a horse's knee high. It didn't stop raining until eleven o'clock. Wellington was in two minds. It was almost the longest day of the year, too. So that he knew, what he missed in the early morning, he could try to make up at the other end of the day. These details were delivered by an excited Anglesey at the monument's peak. Coming almost from the horse's mouth, as it were, it was all the more personal.

'My great-great grandfather drew up his line here . . . Look over there, to your left, do you see that farm? Well, then, late in the day, everybody knackered, blood swilling, horses yelling, out of yonder thunders Blucher . . .'

One could almost have applauded. Indeed, there was, behind me, a small knot of weatherbeaten tourists, dripping in their regulation anoraks, open mouthed at this enthusiastic witness. But then we left for something of a quieter and more chilling nature. The Marquis led me across the now manicured fields to the farmyard at La Huguémont, half a mile from the monument. There were chickens and geese in the near meadow. And cows waiting to be milked, and a man on a tractor, and nobody else.

As Henry Anglesey explained, this is the one spot in that historic landscape that remains unchanged. The walls around the farmland are studded with small square stone memorials, professional tributes from regiments. They record the barest of facts, like a domestic version of the tomb of the Unknown Soldier. But they are equally moving. The bullet holes and cannon marks splatter the still private estate and, most touching of all that remains, a tiny chapel standing at the corner of the farmyard, the door guarded by a white goose, and, inside, a burnt crucifix.

The town of Compiègne lies directly on the road from Waterloo to Paris, and it is historically likely (or possible) that those who had the energy and the money to get that far, came to rest there, in exhaustion and defeat, on the night of the Battle of Waterloo. No harm in imagining that you are now travelling south as part of this ruined band. Dispirited. Dejected. Glad, though, to be beyond the border and home again in France.

It didn't take long in the motor. It was the evening of 30 April and I can remember the date precisely because the town was in late, great bustle. Tomorrow, the First of May and a day for carnival, processions, merry making, fireworks. In most of the countries of mainland Europe, May Day is now a national holiday. In Britain, we are, of course, rather sniffy about a holiday for May Day. It smells of revolution and the possibility, at least, of a demonstration against something or other.

Well, it isn't like that in Compiègne. Or not that I noticed. I was received with unusual fuss and flourish by Madame Boco, the proprietress of Hotel de Harlay, in the centre of the town and on the bank of the River Oise.

If you want to have every preconception of a competent, well-groomed, efficient and flirtatious French Madame truly confirmed, go and call upon her. But don't tell her that I sent you. She is splendid. At every moment of the day, and half into the night, she looks as though she has stepped out of a catalogue advertising the kind of expensive and identifiably colourful clothes they wear in *Dynasty*. The stiletto heel achieves a new dimension when attached to her shoe. She moves swiftly about her business and about yours. She speaks French like someone from an English amateur dramatic society imitating someone speaking French. Exaggerated and very precise. You are *most* welcome. The bedroom is *very* comfortable. There is one tiny hiccup.

'Est-ce qu'il y a une vue de la rivière?'

'Er . . . non, monsieur. J'ai pensé que vous préfériez la silence qu'on peut trouver à l'arrière de notre maison . . . et . . . alors . . . chambre numéro douze.' And no arguing, thank you.

This place isn't like Die Swaene in Bruges. The flowers are profuse and plastic. Information about day trips and museums plaster every wall. The furniture is late Festival of Britain. There is a large ever-beaming colour television upon which everything and everybody is reproduced in pale pastel shades.

There is a maid, who runs all the time, everywhere. Madame, behind the small rampart of her desk, imperiously bangs her palm upon the nozzle of a brass bell. The maid runs from the back room, almost curtseys, picks up your bag – 'No, please, let me' – and runs away with it. You run after her. When you come back down from your 'derrière chambre', with a commanding view of the parking lot and an assortment of Compiègne's higher attics to order tea, bang goes the bell and out rushes Fanny Blankers Koen. She must be a lady in her late fifties. She is as thin as a bean pole. That I can understand. She laughs the whole time. That I cannot.

Tea is taken in a corner of the 'lounge'. The tea things are presented on a tray which has a lace mat. The tray is placed upon a glass table top covered by a lace cloth. The maid's cuffs and neck are trimmed with lace. And just when I thought that, perhaps, I had escaped the pernicious influence of the lace-makers of the Low Countries, here is evidence of their insidious invasions.

I happened to be discussing my inability to come to grips with the problem of lace one night, some months ago, in a cosily reflective mood. 'What', I asked, 'is lace for?'

The company looked at me as though I had swallowed something mildly harmful, something which had temporarily affected my senses. Then a bold father of the church cleared his throat and said, 'Lace is for trimming ladies' cami-knickers. Beyond that I am not prepared to go.' There was universal mirth but no clearer indication of its purpose.

The May Day bells of Compiègne woke me early. 'Wake me early, mother . . .' I took my customary early morning fix of a dip into the Lyttelton-Hart Davis correspondence. I go to sleep, at the other end, with the same tincture. It's so addictive, so reassuring, so wise, funny, sarcastic and learned . . . like all that a good traveller should be, and what I wish I were. May Day is Britten, and the Spring Symphony and a choir cuckoo-ing on top of Magdalen Tower in early morning Oxford. And a similar release of late spring's heady gas infected this part of France too.

This, of course, is Joan of Arc's patch. There are numerous testimonies to her skill in defeating the English. The victory is celebrated in street names, squares, tea shops, garages and a dry cleaners. Fame doesn't really come more universally.

There is, consequently, various competition to be 'Joan' on a float, on May Day. This problem has been overcome with the simplicity, almost naiveté, which characterises the heroine herself. Why one Joan when there are at least thirty carts? The banks, particularly, jump on to this moving wagon. Each bank, and there are plenty, 'proudly presents' their particular Joan.

I spent the day wandering through the streets, stopping at this corner and at that, to witness the preparations. Eleven 'Joans' looked blank at the mention of George Bernard Shaw. One of them, though, did for a celestial moment look as though she was getting voices, and asked if he was a pop star. An adventurous group threw local caution to the winds and decided to parade another hero, Napoleon, through the streets. I told him I'd just left Waterloo. He seemed reasonably uninterested. Then I asked him what he knew that would help me to understand that day's bloody activity in a field to the north of this market. He looked at me as though I had made a vaguely improper suggestion, and the band played on.

When I got back to the Hotel de Harlay, Madame had changed her front-of-house clothing yet again. She arranged her substantial bosom in a vaguely threatening position on top of the front desk, welcomed one home, banged the bell and ordered a bottle of champagne! There's swank for you. I liked Compiègne.

★   ★   ★

The TGV, which has conveyed me and my arrières pensées thus far, arrives in Lyon, from Paris, precisely upon the hour. I am fighting off the odious comparison with another network, slightly irritated by the punctuality of it all, and, at least, *we* got the time right at Waterloo.

Except for one significant digestive hiccup, I found Lyon, surprisingly, entirely congenial. When people say, 'I have nothing against . . . so and so . . .' you know that they mean exactly the opposite, and that they are preparing you for a punch to your perception. Now, somehow, I had imagined that Lyon was going to be something like Manchester. I have nothing against Manchester, God knows; it has been a second comfortable home to me. But when you embark upon a Grand Tour, you don't necessarily want to spend it in a French Manchester. Paris looks at Lyon with great suspicion. Lyon returns the dubious compliment! 'Second City' is, after all, a diminishing title.

Lyon is a surprisingly elegant and spacious place. It is blessed by an accident of geography in that there is a monumental hill in the middle of it. And the Catholic church, never one to miss an obvious opportunity, clamped the Cathedral on top of it. Unlike the capital city (q.v.) which is flat, and operates at eye-level, this place has landmarks in the sky as it were. You can relate to the river and the hill. You (by 'you' I mean 'I') feel as though you know where you are. This makes Lyon, in a way, a theatrical city. When the Pope came, they had a huge laser beam concert, organised and literally orchestrated by Jean-Michel Jarre, the husband of my Parisian lunch companion Charlotte Rampling. For a Grand Tourist, this is becoming a small world. The Pope, by all accounts, enjoyed the stunning spectacle. I presume that in the Vatican library there is a copy of the video tape and the compact disc of that particular evening's majestic celebration.

The Brochiers have copies, if the Vatican erases. Les frères Brochier, the Brochier Bros., have their exceedingly comfortable lives stitched into the fabric of this wealthy city. They manufacture silk. Beautiful, rare silk. Expensive silk. The same silk that for at least three centuries has formed a solid commercial base for the prosperity of the city.

There are two Brochiers. The elder is Jean. He is tall, distinguished and wears well-cut Brooks Bros. jacket and trousers. The shirt is a special sort of Oxford blue and the tie, spotted silk regulation red. He has, in a manner of speaking, grown out of silk and directed himself towards the industrial manufacture of what he loosely calls 'material'. This, I had imagined, might be large bales of cotton for Marks & Spencer's shirts. Or a shipping order for Laura Ashley curtains. It's more intriguing than that. He supervises the making of 'material' which eventually becomes the nose cone of Concorde. When the sensational white aeroplane slaps through the sound barrier and breaks windows and rattles cups on their saucers in far-off lands, it is Jean Brochier who is responsible. He has sharpened the end of that supersonic pencil to fine effect.

Frère Jacques carries on the silken tradition. These days, much of the work is for personal commission. The great

European fashion houses need special stuff for special customers. Jacques Brochier is at hand. There is a kind of guerrilla unit of designers and illustrators and colorists. Christian Dior was a good friend, and not a bad name to have as a business connection.

'He used to telephone, at odd hours. You know, I remember him saying that he was making a special order. He said he wanted something in silk, "brittle in the moonlight and floating in the wind". It was a tall order,' said Jacques.

'I have the same problem with Stevenage,' said Brother Jean.

'Stevenage?' My eyebrows arched in a distant doubt about my own hearing.

'Stevenage. In Hertfordshire. In England.'

'Yes. Yes.' I replied tetchily.

'Where they make the Concorde's nose cone. They gave me similar requests. Big problems which I like.'

I wonder if they had rehearsed this exchange. I cannot look at Concorde now without thinking of something that floats in silver brittle. I think it, and they, enchanting.

One of the reasons for their attraction as a family is that they are wealthy *and* unostentatious. The extended apartment they occupy in Lyon is externally modest. It is not until you move into the rhythm of their universal business success that you realise they are, in many ways, special. The apartment is partly filled with the domestic clutter which occupies any warm family house. But there is a Rodin maquette on one of the mantelpieces; and there are treasures of contemporary French art on the walls. There is also a fussy wrought iron little staircase, and odd unlovely lamps. It is, however, a living and generous confusion. The family is all there. Sisters, their children, aunts, neighbours. And you do not feel that they have foregathered especially for you. There is too much easy intimacy and too little competition for that.

In case you are forming the image that the Brochiers live in a quiet little back street in Lyon, in modest and contained circumstance, let me also tell you that there is a château and a vineyard in Burgundy.

Jean has brought a case of home-bottled Château Briante for us to sample. 'Home bottled' sets up the wrong kind of vibration. There are suggestions of something you may have experimented with from Boots the Chemist. Something you have put under the stairs for seven months. Something you cannot resist testing from time to time. Something to bore the neighbours with. And, finally, something which costs you twenty times more than a bottle of Vin Ordinaire from the selling-out shop.

This stuff isn't that stuff.

This has an attractive personalised label, showing a picture of a handsome house in Burgundy. The picture perfectly reflects the air of confidential restraint which characterises the family.

When the wine flows, opinions bob to the surface and the tongue has a habit of wagging a little more freely.

'Lyon? Paris? How do I compare them? There is no comparison.' This is Jacques speaking.

Jean says, 'Paris is a suburb of Lyon. The people are nice people. Good people, sometimes. But essentially, they are provincial. They have not altogether the right manners. They will rob you. And they don't weave. The difference here is all between Lyon and Marseilles. Here people are hard working. And serious. (This he says with a sarcastic little laugh.) But in Marseilles they laugh a lot. They take life not seriously. But they are not snob. They are snob in Paris. Are you snob?'

I have to take a large gulp of the Briante before I can address myself, dishonestly, to their question and say, with every ounce of dissemblance, 'Non. Absolument. Je ne suis pas snob. Au revoir!'

★   ★   ★

There is very little evidence, in the writings of those who undertook the original Tour, that food was of any special importance. These days, there are hundreds of specially organised food tours. You get into an air-conditioned coach, somewhere north of Paris, and slide from one rosetted Michelin temple to another. Devotion is paid at each halt. The vocabulary of approval is limited, and decreases in exact proportion to the expansion of the belly. If your tour ended in Strasbourg, you could well be mistaken for a local goose

– wide, fat and weary; and your liver chopped and melted and put into a pot as a delicacy for your successors. Awful prospect.

There are new heroes in Europe. It is difficult to remember the name of the French Prime Minister. It is impossible, and hardly worth the while, to memorise the name of the Italian President. Who is the most distinguished general in Belgium? Who is the Swiss Head of State? There are, of course, a handful of clever European dicks who will already have the answers written on one side of a postcard.

No. The new heroes are the chefs and the fashion designers, the footballers and the tennis stars. Paul Bocuse, St Laurent, Maradona, Becker, all currently inhabit the grand new European pantheon.

To pay witness, if not actually tribute to these new demigods, I went to dine at Mionnay, in the suburb of Lyon, at the restaurant of Alain Chapel. It was an intriguing experience, but not one I would want to repeat in a hurry. It does not need me, at this stage, to underline the fact that, in so many circumstances, I travelled as a privileged person. I had been saving myself for this grand meal. I don't mean I had been dieting and reading Hugh Johnson. I mean that, so far, I had been perfectly satisfied with a 'single crossed knife and fork' place. In Ostend, I was reasonably satisfied with chips and fish. In those days, I was maintaining positive links with the homeland.

Chapel's restaurant is on a main road running out of Lyon. It doesn't look that big a deal from the outside. It looks, in fact, rather like an American roadhouse situated in a well-to-do suburb of Boston. Long and low. Shutters and canopies. The sort of place where you quickly realise that there's a great deal more to it than meets the cursory eye. Chapel invokes immediate feelings of a holy house, which this is. A very well, if autocratically run house. Rich. Organised. There seems little room for any kind of personal expression. The visitor, the diner, the supplicant, the congregation are all required to observe the unspoken and unwritten rituals of the place.

I think there are three broad categories of eating houses. There are those places where you feel warm and expansive and unchallenged and at home. Your own home, that is. Then there are those difficult locations, advertised in rather a silly fashion, as being someone else's lovely untouched home where you will be made to feel welcome. It's always 'we' who do the organising. 'We want you to use the place as though it were your own. Our lovely (who, in their right mind would admit that their own home was 'lovely'?) home is entirely at your disposal. Please feel free.' You can't feel free when you don't know where the lavatory is. You can't feel at all free if you have a sudden urge to make a cup of tea, or need a quick slug of the hard stuff. And if you spill something on the carpet, you can't keep your foot on the stain, hiding it, for more than three or four minutes, or the proprietors ('we') will think you've taken root. 'If you have to go out, please take the front door key with you. We'll be in bed by eleven.' You know what that means. It means that 'we' hope that, if you have to go out, you don't make a noise when you get back.

Then there is the third category. The holy houses. Like Alain Chapel's. The ceremony, for such it is, is precisely timed. The table, or altar, is lit by new candles and fresh flowers. The altar cover is of stiff rich linen. The instruments of service, knives, forks, spoons, are geometrically arranged. The napkin, with which any humble communicant will wipe the corners of his grateful mouth, is usually arranged into the shape of a mystical fan. Sometimes a sacrificial swan. You must not touch it. An altar boy will materialise and ritualistically robe you in this sub-garment of service. The form and order of prayer is delivered with a consequent flourish. It is called the menu. Much of it is incomprehensible like an original Latin Mass. You don't have to translate the words. They will, mystically, be made flesh. Or fowl. Or good red herring. It's interesting that a server is a server, either at this table, or at High Mass. The pervasion of the holy atmosphere ensures a hushed tone to the night's solemn activity. Nobody is laughing uproariously. No one, as far as I can tell, is telling a joke, or swearing, or drunk, or over-amorous. Everyone is in their Whit-Sunday best. I know it's harsh but I have to say that it is intimidating. How do I say, 'Which fork?' Thank God I have learned to hold it properly.

There is even a moment when what I presume is the main course is brought to the table underneath a silver dome. I have seen the relics of saints suddenly displayed, at a maximum theatrical moment, in order to astonish, to frighten even, those whose faith may be wavering. Transubstantiation has often a mortifying effect. 'Voici le poulet estragon!' We have not mentioned wine. Fortunately, the virtue of this glass, at my hand, quickly replenished, is that eventually it will dull the sense of embarrassment and embolden me to cope (bishop's dress) with the arrival of the chariot of desserts. At such a time, I shall have moved to a higher spiritual plane, where doubt, question and uncertainty are not entertained. And that, after all, is the ultimate purpose of so profound an experience.

Except, and this is a most shocking exception, except that, as an appetiser, as an organ voluntary in a church, at that moment when you are settling into the pew, clearing your throat, taking the measure of congregation, I was offered an unidentifiable little dish. A sort of hors d'oeuvres of the house. The first mouthful was delicious. After the second, I began to wonder about the composition and the character of the concoction, on its comfortable bed of lightly toasted bread.

'It is the semen of carp,' announced M. Chapel. Now, this intelligence produces one of two possibilities. Either you put down your knife and fork and make a strenuous effort to call the Fisheries Protection Service. Or you decide that, maybe, it is coming time to move on.

Your Grand Tourist had, in many years gone by, to face all kinds of terrors, threats, personal assaults, robbers, pickpockets and brigands. I dare swear that they never had to dispose of carp's semen. For that matter, I can't imagine how the carp disposed of it. Nevertheless, this was my last (and you will not be surprised to hear) lasting image of Lyon.

In the same olden days, the Tourist had to make an important decision in his thrust to the South. He could either turn left and head to the Alps, mount his way into Switzerland, and proceed in that path which Hannibal and Bernard Levin have both immortalised. Or, he could drive south, to the shore of the Mediterranean, hail a passing felucca, and be wafted in warmish water to Genoa and to an Italian landfall. That was then. This is now. The airport at Lyon has a reasonable service to Berlin where I am, again assuming the humble manner of a baton, to be picked up by John Wells, my next conductor, my next guide. He will, hopefully, have things to show me and tales to tell. And, putting down my knife and fork and uttering a silent prayer, I will surely have things to tell him.

Appetiser of carp's semen. Lyon

CHAPTER
THREE

I shall tell you what the 'Grand Tour' has done for me so far. It has confirmed some prejudices and confounded others. Hitherto, I had believed myself to be an inveterate Francophile, and that is no longer what Dame Edna Everage calls 'the bottom line'. I have, for instance, re-formed my ideas about Paris, which, if you can read between these narrow lines, you will have already noted. Germany, apart that is from changing planes inside Frankfurt International Airport, I have never encountered. The language is as the full walls of hieroglyphs on an Egyptian pyramid. Meaningless and, apart from the odd similarity, unintelligible.

The Germans, throughout my impressionable childhood, were the enemy. My Granny Harty told me that, just before 1914, there were lots of brass bands from Hamburg and Berlin, walking up and down the streets of Blackburn, Lancashire, always with a little man with a notebook, whose job it was to mark down the names of streets, the numbers of houses, and the position of the Town Hall. Not an efficient way of spying. And so typically and blatantly Germanic. I believed her. I saw one flying bomb, in 1944, sailing with a single deadly drone through the dark blue sky of a late winter evening, and heading towards Preston. I thought, or more precisely, was told, that this was an outrage, and that we should not forgive these people. I hadn't worked out, in my simple mind, whether it was outrageous *per se*, or an outrage because the target was Preston.

Hitler was the bogey man. I can hear my mother giving my sister a sharp slap, and telling her that if she didn't go to sleep when she was told, Adolf would come and get her. We had a large street party after VJ Day. We abandoned the air-raid shelters and all the redolent smells of sacrificial candles and concrete sprayed by four years of dog pee. It wasn't until I grew to be of a more discerning and suspicious age that I began to understand the horrors of the concentration camp. That, sadly, as it now stands, served simply to put a hard seal upon my prejudice. I did not like Germans. I would not like Germany.

I flew into West Berlin with John Wells, my guide to the city. He used to teach in Germany. He has an envious fluency in this strange language. I told him everything I've told you. About fear and suspicion. The first thing we saw as we came along the flight corridor which connects West Berlin to the rest of West Germany, was the hard white line of the Wall. 'Something there is that does not love a wall.' And this wall, that stands between a father's house and his child's, dominates the whole feeling, thought and individuality of the city.

John Wells is both the best and the worst kind of guide. Best, because he is enthusiastic, and knowledgeable and, being who he is, amusing. Worst, because he runs everywhere. He is born out of the same gene as the maid in Compiègne. He never strolls. He hardly ever walks. He is like a squash ball on heat, banging against the walls of the city.

We dived into a beer cellar. I was given a quick trip through the ordered maze of the language. Words, apparently, are bolted on to other words so that a vast and complicated concept can be reduced to a very long word. A portmanteau. 'Except', as Wells said, 'Christopher Isherwood managed very well with "Guten Tag" and "Hello, sailor".'

I was instructed not to ignore the importance of rules. There are rules for many things. Rules at traffic lights. Rules about the side you take in walking into the underground. Queueing rules. Rules in restaurants. Even, God help us, rules about pornography. Nude magazines have rules about breasts and other sensitive areas. Things (as it were) are frequently carried too far. A vast exaggeration prevails. It is not a question of overstatement. It is simply an insurance policy. Breasts must be big breasts, very big, in case you thought they were simply pimples.

Armed with this essential social ammunition, one felt ready to go into the streets. In truth, there is little to go into the streets of West Berlin for. You may as well walk up and down Kensington High Street and pretend that you are abroad. The shops glitter. The street lights shine. Taxis cruise. Buses stop. The people are well heeled. The architecture is heavy, wholesome and unadventurous. West Berlin is, at the end of every day, a privileged and wealthy playground, unconnected with the immediate harsh realities of the communist bloc.

There is, of course, the Wall. That came later.

Mr Wells conveyed me to the East. You go through a rigorous and eventually tedious screening process at Checkpoint Charlie. A Wagnerian maiden scrutinises the underside of your vehicle, with a mirror on the end of a long pole. It is, in some ways, like a giantess working in a dentist's surgery, making a preliminary check with her exaggerated equipment.

We passed, without problem, to the Palasthotel – all one word – in the Karl Liebenechtstrasse. Dear 'something' street. It was not what I had been led to expect. At least, I thought, we shall be staying in a dormitory, or a cell, or a dimly lit guest house. No fear. The front doors, which slide effortlessly as you break the control beam, are plastered with a list of acceptable credit cards. Visa, American Express, Diners and what not. All the easy financial sliproads to instant credit. Fully accepted and very acceptable.

The front desk betrays the inner aridity of it all. There are long racks, where your key should be hanging, and where any messages would be left. But that kind of business is conducted out of your sight and under their desks. The bar could be lifted out of the East, and lowered, on a wire, into the West and nobody would know the difference. They shake a whisky sour with the best. The climate is air-controlled. The elevators are in good working order. You need to pinch yourself occasionally, to remind yourself that you are in the grim and forbidding East.

Look at the hotel bedroom. There's a mini-bar. There are extra pillows in the cupboard. There's shoe-cleaning material. There's even, in the best and most efficient Hilton tradition, an ice-dispenser in the corridor. Seven channels on the television, two of them from the West. You must not, of course, use the words East and West. Here you are in Berlin, thank you very much. What the people over the Wall choose to call it is their problem, their responsibility. That kind of head-on thinking gives you rather a lurch.

It was not until I was lying in a hot bath in the Palasthotel, thinking that, well . . . maybe . . . the East is the East and the West hasn't got it entirely together, anyway. Looking forward to a night out with John Wells, who had threatened, if not promised, a surprise. Suddenly, I was jerked out of this reverie by a dreadful gurgling sound. I watched the level of my soapy bathwater begin to drop. Then I looked out, and saw the same bathwater rising, in direct proportion, upon the bathroom floor. Clearly, I was not connected to the most efficient waste unit in Europe. And, equally clearly, there are cracks in the domestic, if not the political, systems of the East. I called the front desk. They didn't want to know. Towels and squeezing took eventual care of the swamp.

'Schadenfreude', a lightening of the spirit at the expense of another's misery, threatened to overtake me. Did, in fact. Nobody, I thought, is perfect. Until I met Mr Wells, in the desert-like lobby of the hotel. For goodness knows what reason, he had to appear as Denis Thatcher. Slightly tight-fitting suit. Clean shirt. A tie with not the sharpest of knots. Hair wet, and plastered into conference party contours.

We arrived, by taxi, in a gloomy back street of East Berlin. The driver pointed to a dark alley, and we had difficulty finding our way to the front door of the Ballhaus. I had been told what to expect, but that was in broad outline. The details made the picture different. It is a dance hall, in so much as there is a floor and a band. The floor is sprung and polished like some of the customers. There are balconies, on two levels, around the rectangle of the floor. There are tables, each seating four people, most of them occupied by two. And at the end of each table there is an old-fashioned telephone, underneath a large white round globe of an electric light upon which is painted the number of your particular table. When you have settled down, and been served, you wait. If you are young, handsome, attractive, you won't have to wait long before the telephone rings. When you answer it, a proposition will be made.

'Would you like a drink?'

'Would you like to dance?'

'Would you like to go for a walk?'

'Would you like to come home for coffee?'

'Would you like to make the night hideous with carousing?'

'Would you like to go to Potsdam on a weekend saver ticket?'

'Would you care to spend the rest of your life with me?'

All you have to do with any of these alternatives is to ask what number is calling.

'22,' is the reply.

Then you scan the floor, search the tiers, and fix your critical gaze on '22'. The answer to any or all of these fundamental questions is entirely at your discretion. It is, of course, a much more dangerous game than that you play sitting in your Parisian café, counting every seventh person. Here, you are confronted with the real thing, and you have to push your mind into the gear of a user-friendly computer. It has to work rapidly. There is no maybe.

There is, however, a significant alternative. There is another end to most telephones. I mean, you can take the initiative. You can do the searching. This, of course, does not guarantee that the number won't be engaged.

Now, the surprising detail of this questionable arrangement is that a passable air of wholesomeness prevails. Written down, in the manner of a guide book, you would conclude that here is a rather seedy knocking shop – a place for vagrants, deviants, the hungry, the thirsty and those with 'no home to go to' as they say of the doubtful folk in the North of England.

Not at all. It's lively; it's lighthearted; there are jokes; there

Ballhaus. East Berlin. Busy line.

is a complete lack of embarrassment. It is, at a pinch, the sort of place you could take your mother to. For someone addicted to booze, company and the telephone, it must be near to heaven. The phone calls are, incidentally, free. The beer is pricey.

Mr Wells took me to rather too prominent a position. I swear to God that we had scarcely arranged ourselves in this heady landscape when the telephone tinkled above the exuberance of the band. Some fit of immodesty led me to believe that it would be for me. I snatched at the receiver. An East German voice, silky and persuasive, eventually gave me to understand that it was the other gentleman she wished to engage. Wells-as-Thatcher took the instrument and began to behave like the worried hero of a spy movie. The telephone cradled under his chin, one hand with seeming nonchalance on his glass, his eyes narrowing into a furtive search of the Ballhaus. A quick nod. A sealed deal, and off he went to whisk some elegant Frau through the paces of whatever is the Communist equivalent of the Valeta.

It's not easy to be deserted so early in the evening by the lifeguard. I couldn't deal with the orders when the girl came to ask what else we would drink. I certainly could not deal with the telephone if it ever were to jerk itself into the ringing sounds of an invitation. Which is, of course, exactly what happened. I struggled with the language, and tried to adopt a carefree posture. But I couldn't locate the caller until I felt an urgent little tap on my back. It was my putative partner. I felt suddenly like a million dollars. I began to understand a little of the marginally decadent charm and romance of Berlin. The night club scene, I have to confess, I find totally resistible. Licensed naughtiness tends not to be naughty enough. Sally Bowles and Isherwood, and all that daring pre-war razmattazz, leave me loosely unconcerned.

Nothing untoward, you will be happy to hear, came out of this novel experience. Twenty-seven into 22 won't go. Even if you carry one – and one was, indeed, being expertly carried.

By the next dawn's early light, we were up and about before the streets were properly aired. Running, as usual. Wells in his speedy enthusiasms for the Eastern sector of Berlin.

'There's a real feeling, when you cross over the border, that you're going into a sort of spy novel. But the odd thing about East Berlin is that it's much more authentically German simply because it hasn't been prostituted by American capitalism. Because they've had no money in the East, all the old buildings have been slightly mended, slightly put right. So you still have a rather strong atmosphere. But the really interesting thing is, I think, that most West Berliners have a kind of sneaking regard and envy of the East Berliners. I think it's because they feel as though they live in a really wicked city, whereas over there, it isn't so much that they're communist; it's really that they are kind of Puritans.

'I was a clergyman's son, and we used to have evangelical meetings where people said, "All will go well if only we have God helping us." The same goes in East Berlin with "the Party". It's "the Party" that stops them advertising; stops rampant capitalism; stops pornographic cinemas; stops dizzy behaviour with stocks and shares. They are the inheritors of the German Protestant past!'

You can see exactly what Mr Wells means when we arrive panting at the door of the vast Pergamon Museum in East Berlin. It looks like the British Museum but, somehow, raised on stilts. Its grand classical façade is half-hidden by a brutal Nazi addition, but the rest of it is solidly eighteenth-century Berlin, with a heavy hint of Prussia about it.

Inside, it is breathtaking. Just before we dashed through the front hall, John Wells paused to call upon the imagination again, to remind me what this place must have looked like in 1945. Then, the outside must have been chaotic, and slapped by the heavy bombardment. Even now, there are great shell holes in the brick walls. And bullet holes signed like angry graffiti along the sides. At that time, there were ruins outside and ruins within.

According to my guide, the place tells you more about Germany than it does about Greece. The remains of a massive Greek temple, in part restored, give you an idea of what the Germans thought a Greek temple should look like. It is, in part, a saluting base. An altar. A platform from which you could declare war, or upon which you could award medals, badges of honour, flags, favours.

'This is an intelligent Disneyland, you know,' confides Mr
Wells, as we march, in triumph, through the Babylonian
Gate of Ishtar. 'A lot of it is discreetly restored. But nothing
is hidden away. Nothing reduced from its superhuman scale,
and the guards don't fire on you if you happen to lean against
a three thousand year old wall.'

It is understandably grand. Walking through temples and
arches, staring at vast columns, squinting at heads on plinths
can eventually lead you to that kind of indigestion you get
when you are searching in the big tin can of superlatives that
you must carry on your back. You've seen people on food
programmes on television. They suffer an awful lot.
Someone opens an oven door, and pulls out a steaming dish
of something that has taken half a light year and a pint of
cream to prepare. You are the guest taster. You say 'Oooh!
It's delicious,' and then the cook presents you with a second
dish. 'Oooh, it's delicious.' Then, a third. 'Oooh! This *is* delicious,' wiping a drooling mouth. Then she says, 'If you
think that's delicious, and you've said so, you wait until I
take out the chef d'oeuvre. Now, that *is* delicious.' Then
you are presented with another steaming casserole.
'Mmmmmm! This is *de*-licious.' And on it grinds, all trace of
elements of sincerity now long evaporated.

In just such a grindingly appreciative manner are we
required to behave in the Pergamon Museum. And, Jove
knows, it is most certainly not the considerable size and
standard of these treasures which ultimately flattens the
excitement of your response. It is that you are drained,
exhausted and bombarded with such spectacle.

I often wonder what would happen if Miss Melina Mer-
couri, in her capacity as Minister of Culture, called in at the
Office of Culture, here in East Berlin, and said, 'We want
our ruins, and our marbles, and everything back; and we're
not going home until we get them.' Somebody would have
to take her to a Greek restaurant, so that she could smash a
plate or two in this frustrating outburst. The problem is,
there are no local Greek restaurants.

Tourists need light relief. Either that, or what the bro-
chures call 'Afternoon free for last minute shopping'. Shopping is a mindless occupation. If I want one thing which I can

reasonably afford, then I will buy it. Throughout the length of this Grand Tour, I saw only one thing I wanted, and I bought six of them. Five to give away, and one which I have placed inside a kind of home-made tabernacle. I'll tell you about that when I get there.

John Wells took me to lunch and light relief at the zoo. When God created the dromedary, he had a universal plan at hand. Therefore, a dromedary in an East Berlin zoo looks exactly like a dromedary anywhere else. No one holds back their hands in terrible exclamation to say 'Oh, look, there's a communist dromedary!'

We stood in a patient queue for sausages and beer. Undistinguished food. But we sat in a spacious park, and there were lots of children making non-specific communist noises; and their parents looked ordinary; and the sun shone; and sparrows came to peck at leftovers.

Mr Wells went there fifteen years ago. He had an hour or so to kill before he went to the Opera. He was wearing a smart suit, like the one he wore to the night club last night. He wandered through the parklands of the zoo, and when he was staring at some gibbons, being more than just comradely, he heard a suspicious German voice saying something in colloquial phraseology. When he worked this out, with the aid of a friend, and a dictionary, the rude communist had said, 'Look at him, what's he come as?' Today he was not wearing his zoo-suit!

Checkpoint Charlie is, perhaps, the most popular venue on the tourist route. The Wall is broken by the attendant militia. You go through two checks. This way – that is returning from the East to go back to West Berlin – the Communist check is rigorous. Lots of papers to be examined. Guards, with slow-moving scrutiny.

One starts to behave as guiltily as passing through a customs check. One has absolutely nothing to declare, nothing to be frightened of. But that is the straightforward voice of reason. Reason is the need to escape from what has been, and still (let us not kid ourselves) is, a harsh and repressive regime. Reason is what people, all along the Wall and all along the corridor of time, since this barrier was erected, have died for.

As you pass away from the East German guard and on through the American sector, you see brighter lights, and advertisements for Marlborough cigarettes, and all the commercial glitter of the capitalist West. Make no mistake. Responses are not, in this place, simple and straightforward. 'Without sharp east, without declining west.'

Yes, I am glad to be going back to what I vaguely understand as freedom. No, I am not untouched by the ideas which have faced me for the first time. I know quite well, but deep down and not bubbling on any expressive surface, what John Wells means by a 'religion', a 'restraint', a 'discipline', a situation in which you are less important than the sum of the parts which compose the 'State'. Of course I am too selfish, too powered by money, by acquisitions, by controlled greed (and sometimes by uncontrollable greed), by the pomps and vanities of this wicked world, and the engineered lusts of the West. And yet, why are these walls not covered with nasty graffiti? Why are the windows in the telephone kiosk not broken? Is it, simply, because you would be sent to Siberia if you were a noticeable vandal? Is it that simple?

It is curious that the first person I talked to, back in the comfortable garish sofa of the West, was a young border guard who had recently defected from the confines of that land I had just left. I met Ralf within spitting distance of the Wall, in the café underneath the Checkpoint Charlie Museum. This building is a small, highly eloquent testimony to the courage of those who, in their own terms, escaped. They escaped in the cramped boot of a mini. They fled by balloon, by tunnel, by disguise, by hanging on the inside of a van roof, by clinging to a piece of wood in a canal, and by various other foolhardy but necessary methods. The latest exhibit is a powered hang-glider. Useful, and sporting, if designed for one person floating on the thermals of a warm afternoon above the limestone escarpments of North Yorkshire. A different story if this flimsy toy is required to power a family to freedom.

Ralf is, maybe, twenty-four. I never asked his age. It didn't seem important. He was an East German border guard, in one of those ugly high boxes that stand at every corner or geometrical break in the line of the Wall. He was trained for two years in East Germany. He wouldn't tell me where. Far from Berlin. When 'they' thought he was ready, he was sent to the Wall, for guard duty. For the first two months, he looked for the right place to escape. There are two guards each day and each night in each tower. They change one person every twelve hours, so that you never mount guard with the same person for more than one twelve-hour period in your entire service. If you spent too much time with one other person you could, heaven help us, become his friend. He would then know too much, or more dangerously, pretend to know too little.

Ralf, in full uniform and with a loaded gun, went to his twelve-hour duty acting a part. He went to meet his fellow, and acted the part of a buffoon. A serious buffoon. Shadow boxing, playing the kind of game that mindless rugger teams play after a match. Stupid, almost. 'Come on. Put 'em up. Are you a man or a mouse?' After two or three hours of this non-transparent sparring, his fellow guard grew used to Ralf's apparently adolescent activity. Bear in mind that neither Ralf nor his guard had anything by which to compare this odd behaviour. This twelve-hour enforced and close confinement would happen only once, and that fact Ralf kept a hold of.

When he screwed his courage to the sticking place, he punched his mate, grabbed hold of his arms and slipped on handcuffs smartly, from behind. He locked him to the door. The fellow guardee thought it was a joke. It was not. It was serious.

'Did you tell anybody you were planning this?'

'No. You cannot tell anyone. It is dangerous for yourself and it is very good for the Secret Service in East Germany. If your friends know, then they are in big danger . . . bigger danger than you.'

'Did you have friends who tried to escape?'

'Nobody.' Categorical.

'I am the first from my friends.'

'Are you being diplomatic?'

'Maybe.'

I don't think it would do me, or Ralf, any good in pursuing this line. He did what he did. He is comfortably accommodated in the West. He seems happy. He is intelligent. He is now a student of history and sociology – what else! He has been recently on a holiday to Venice. He has spoken to his family, once, by telephone. He knew that what he was saying was being overheard. His story is by no means unique. Simply that, on this journey, with all its licensed freedom, it was a salutary meeting, an immediate history lesson, and a time for a few moments of reflection.

★　　★　　★

Every seemingly grey communist cloud has a silver lining. I left West Berlin in a coach, to rejoin the southern dynamic of the Grand Tour. There is little to detain me in the city. The people are prosperous and busy. So are the shops. Also the hotels. People urgently about their business do not always make the most entertaining society.

I bade a breathless farewell to John Wells, and looked forward to a slump, and a snooze in a coach ride from West Berlin to Hamelin. I had forgotten that once we came to the outskirts of the city we would be locked again into the strict rules of the East. There is a long, straight, tedious ribbon of motorway which eventually draws you back into West Germany. So many quick demographic shocks in so short a time and space. Checks, customs, ladies with mirrored geiger counters, all that paraphernalia yet again.

Half way along the road corridor, driving in a strictly regulated low-speed zone, I asked if we could stop to go to the lavatory at the next road house. The answer was a firm 'No'. There is only one place you can do that. Half way along the route. It looks like a road house from somewhere in the deserted mid–West of America. Two petrol pumps; a lavatory and, next door, a shop full of useless articles for the hungry traveller – things like ghetto blasters and perfume with powerfully punched names like 'Clash' and 'Thrust'. I bought an ice-cream and a packet of the East German equivalent of Smarties, and the coach moved.

At the other interminable end of the motorway, yet more officialdom to yawn your way through. This is where I caught sight of a silver lining. I was gazing through the big window at rows of international trucks waiting to be cleared, when up alongside came a coach-load of tourists from Garstang, in Lancashire, half an hour from where I live. I blinked at the name. They blinked at me. Then there began a furious waving, and mouthing of messages, all of us behaving as though we were shouting above the noise of cotton looms in our native patch. Lancastrians call this method of communication 'mee-mowing'. You mee-mo at me and I mee-mo back at you, and the whole process is infinitely more rewarding when you actually do it than when you have to write it down.

I asked the guard who was combing our coach if I could leave and go to talk with the cheerful neighbours in the next lane. No. That was not allowed. Nor were they allowed to leave to come and talk to me.

It may be a trivial conclusion. That I wouldn't deny. But my most vivid image of the unnecessarily repressive nature of the East German regime is that of one coach-load trying to communicate with another. And laughing a lot in the process. The chief topic of our interchange was to do with the best place to buy Lancashire cheese. There is a popular television game called *Give Us A Clue*. I watch it. I even play in it. The Garstang crowd clearly understood the private grammar of the game, too. The guards were bemused but not amused by the inane silent occupation of two coach-loads, just within their territory, miming their own business. With faithful cross-promises to meet for a reunion drink in the Golden Crown, near Lancaster, we crossed the border in our separate coaches – they towards the beckoning smell of cheese, and I to unknown parts of Germany.

★   ★   ★

Hamelin town's in Brunswick,
By the famous Hanover City.
The River Weser, deep and wide,
Washes its walls on the southern side.

There is little point in refusing to be a middle-of-the-road, down-the-line, join-the-crowd, we've-come-here-to-enjoy-ourselves tourist. One can get quite grand and huffy about searching out secret parts, scratching in private territories, ushered in red-lined privilege to the places where no ordinary traveller might hope to go. But then, there are other paths which might be well-trodden for a very good reason.

I drove into Hamelin in despondent mood. On my own, more or less, in a land whose language I could neither speak nor write.

And, suddenly, you find yourself in the right mood for this kind of city. The place, this place, cheers you. There is a friendly air. There are exquisite houses, built in the middle ages, a little over-decorated for my taste, higgledy-piggledy streets, a wide river, little feeling of the twin Berlin oppressions of commercialism and communism.

The taste of a place, the Zeitgeist, hovers so delicately above it. A puff of critical wind, a slight seismic shift, even a depression or a hangover, and one's perceptions change. Somehow, those who have been responsible for restoring the town, for making it a home fit for a piper, and rats, and children, has just about got it right. The possibilities of riotous and offensive tweedom have been delicately avoided.

The Piper is a handsome and intelligent figure. He dresses in a red and yellow costume, with a pointed Robin Hood hat and proud pheasant feathers, and he plays the oboe. Twice a day, in the season, and on festive occasions, he successfully performs a little miracle. He walks down the cobbled streets of Old Hamelin, piping and fluting. Out of doorways and alleys, a little hesitantly, with their tails in the shape of question marks, come the rats. Munching, nibbling, squeal-

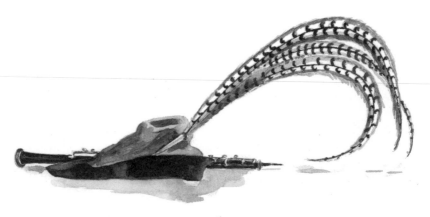

ing little things. The Piper spirits them away to the edge of the town, where they whip off their costumes, jump into a bus, and are returned to the starting post in order to change into the dress of medieval children. They are led, again, in a band, looking like a glum collective of deprived youth, until they disappear away over the horizon.

The only thing I have failed to suggest is the charm of it all. On paper, it does rather read like the kind of event one would willingly make a considerable detour to avoid. In the squeaking, piping and colourful flesh, it is an entertaining half hour of European mythology.

It being the latter half of the twentieth century, it came as no surprise to hear that the Pied Piper had taken the rats and kids on long-haul flights to Canada and Japan. Herr Sacher, the Piper, is a professional musician. He has to be. Part of his wages are paid by the City Council. Sometimes he has to lead tourists from the boats which dock on the river, and transport the bemused masses to that part of the town where there are financial incentives. No question of spiriting them off into a magical mountain or mysteriously urging them to found a new race in a new land in the East.

Today there is a plague of pigeons in the city centre. They are peckingly unconcerned with the sound of his pipe.

The Piper's eyes brighten at the mention of Rentokil. 'They have been here. They are commercial. They are like me. They get rid of rats. But they do not bring tourists. You have not come here to see how Rentokil works, have you?'

No, Herr Sacher. I haven't.

★   ★   ★

Germany is now beginning to make sense. Sense in humour, that is. At least the Pied Piper had heard of Rentokil and we managed to make a spirited contact without the use of flattening Esperanto. Maybe his great-grandfather played in the German band just before the First World War, and wrote down my Granny Harty's address in order that the Zeppelin would find her two-up, two-down, and flatten her.

My Granny Harty was born in 1866, and she imitated Queen Victoria in almost every way except language. When the Germans came over Blackburn in 1941, and she was beginning to be an old lady, I was sent to her bedroom to persuade her to come down to the air-raid shelter. I cried to her and she said, 'If God wants me this night, he must take me in my bed. And I've just let my hair down for the night. So bugger Hitler.' The world, the flesh and the devil disposed of in one ripe mouthful. Her commands and decisions were as final in our household as Queen Victoria's in hers.

Now that I am in more confident German stride, and hesitating to become over-confident and goose-stepped, I have turned towards Coburg, to the home of Prince Albert, the Prince Consort, the beloved husband of Queen Victoria.

I have Stanley Weintraub's biography of Victoria in my suitcase, and that has told me more about the Queen's visceral nature than I had hitherto suspected. I fell under the influence of Victoria when I fell under the spell of Cecil Woodham-Smith. When Mrs Woodham-Smith was engaged in the research of her biography of the Imperial Queen, she used to travel by train from London to Windsor. At lunch time, the Librarian insisted that the building should be closed, so the frail and strikingly elegant Mrs Woodham-Smith walked out of the Castle, down to the Railway Station, took a seat in the waiting room, unwrapped her thinly sliced smoked salmon sandwiches, took a sip from her flask and watched the hands of the big clock wind on to two. Then, having been an extraordinary lady-in-waiting, she returned to her literary duties at the Castle. Now I am confusing Cecil Woodham-Smith with Queen Victoria and Granny Harty as I slide into Coburg.

My first appointment is with Prince Andreas von Saxe-Coburg and Gotha. Now, there's a name to conjure with. It may not be as chic as Pirelli, but it sure as hell sells almanacs. Prince Andreas came to my hotel to collect me and take me to dinner on the night of my arrival. I peeped through the hotel bedroom window eager to witness the arrival of the Royal entourage. Coach? Black-plumed horses? Rolls Royce? Bodyguard?

A metallic new Range Rover, the Prince at the wheel, conveyed me to the restaurant. We sat around a comfortable table in front of a roaring and spitting fire. The service was fine, but I had the feeling that sitting with Prince Albert's great-great grandson, a direct descendant, did not impede the smartness of the presentation or the speediness of the delivery.

I have discovered, so far into my travels, that planned meetings do not necessarily unroll, like well cut and patterned wallpaper, exactly as you had supposed. You can lie in bed, snooze in a train or tap the speculative wheel of your car, and make all kinds of imaginative forecasts of the encounter you are about to make. Prince Andreas, for instance, will tell me stories about Prince Albert. I shall discover, or even uncover, little family secrets which will add bumps and muscle to already recorded history.

No such thing.

Prince Andreas is more interested in his young and growing trees, in the forests of the neighbouring estates, and in the land he has recently acquired in the West of Scotland, than in the ossified genealogies of middle Europe. He speaks with an American accent, on account of being educated there, and having an American step-father. He dresses in the manner of a successfully anonymous business man with a house in Martha's Vineyard, and a smart office on Lexington and 34th.

An agitated waiter came bumbling to the side of the table and muttered something in rapid German. I knew it was for me but could make neither head nor tail of this intelligence. He indicated to Prince Andreas that two suspicious people at the table in the far corner wanted me to go to speak with them. Sometimes this kind of thing happens, and then they apologise and say that they thought you were someone else (nearly always Des O'Connor). I begged leave to be excused from the princely presence, but took my napkin as a kind of signal that I was still a part of the host's table. That is a useful part of the body language of lifelines.

'My name's Jeff Orford. I believe you know Irene Chatburn; she's always at your sister's house in Blackburn.'

Tell me how you explain to Prince Albert's great-great grandson that you have acquaintances sitting in his ancestral town who know somebody, who knows somebody else, who's auntie used to clean for them. It's one thing to be lying in bed, planning the elegant route of the Grand Tour, trimming your fantasy with every conceivable social bauble, as

Albert taught Victoria to trim her first Christmas tree. It is quite another to be so vigorously reminded of the diminutive proportions of this village called 'The World' which we all inhabit.

A restful night's sleep in Coburg. Radio 4 has lost its temporary attractions. Tomorrow morning I shall not make an attempt to buy yesterday's *Times* at Coburg Railway Station. Is there the faintest hint of independence here? I am going to behave like a tourist again. I shall find Prince Albert, on his pedestal in the Square. I shall read the inscription which tells me, here in my touristic bedroom, that Queen Victoria came back in 1865 to unveil this proud memorial to her husband. She paid for it, too, and that matters. She brought the family. She paid for them. She stayed next door, in the Ehrenburg Palace, where traditional little stories remain constant in a part of the patter of the guides.

'The Queen was a big little round lady . . .' So proclaimed the guide. 'When she came to unloose the statue, she could not climb the stairs of the Palace, and so she pulled up, or wound up, along that shaft (pointing to a bulge in the corner) here, to the second floor, where she could then move.'

We moved to another grand room, with a large bed in it.

'Above the bed is a picture of Windsor Castle. That was to make the Queen feel as though she was at home. Look. Here is a bust of Queen Victoria when she was a child . . . about eight or nine . . . and then, opposite, a little statue of the Queen as the Empress of India.'

Interesting, one observes, that the older and more important you become, the smaller they need to make your statue.

'And here, in this corner, is the first water closet installed on the continent of Europe by Queen Victoria. She refused to stay here until it was installed!'

What an odd rate of exchange in the social currency of the nineteenth century. While Coburg gave Britain a Prince Consort the Queen gave Coburg its first lavatory. One PC equals one WC.

CHAPTER
FOUR

I can forget 'The War', but I can't forgive the makers of
mechanical clocks. I arrived in gentle good humour in
Munich, after my peaceful encounters with Victoria and
her Albert. I parked the car and strolled into the central
square. 'Great was my amazement,' as Dean Swift would
have put it, 'to discover a milling crowd of people in silent
admiration or expectation.'

There were lots of them. Fellow-travellers and Bavarian
locals in hats with brushes, and Lederhosen, gazing in stupe-
faction at the side of the Town Hall. Nothing was happening. I searched out a bold American lady who seemed to
understand the significance of this non-ritual.

'They are waiting for noon,' she announced.

'Noon?'

'At noon, a lot of mechanical dolls will come out of that
hole and travel round, banging things.'

'It is only twenty minutes to twelve,' I said.

'Yes, but people come from all corners of the world to see
this truly wonderful display. I can't understand how you've
never heard of it.'

Twenty wasted minutes. I slithered into the position of a
wondering, gawping wanderer. I stared and stared. I pressed
time to move more quickly, and then, with unmelodic

clonkings and bongings, this heavy Germanic performance began. 'Performance' is too generous a word to use here. Knights and their ladies, one at a time, revolved in leaden procession, around a balcony. The audience made baleful noises of appreciation which petered out after three or four minutes, but still the relentless mechanisms propelled these permanent burghers of Munich. Lord, how tired they must be. How pointless their existence. And were they, I wondered, at any moment looking down upon the upturned faces of an eager crowd, the crowd perhaps fluctuating but the faces forever changeless, and thinking the same? Their life was a ceaseless round, rather like bored night-clubbers in London.

All that apart, I like Munich. There's no East and West Munich, the city is busy, but not hysterical. There is space. There is some decent residual grandeur. For those who should desire, there are shops, and elegant ones they are, too. But all these characteristics are to be found in 200 or 2,000 cities, and it will be clear, by this middling stage, that I am more excited by the inhabitants than by their monuments.

I am particularly intrigued by reports of a girl from Beckenham, who has put down an odd root in this supposedly raunchy city, and has made a success of what they call, in modern guide books, a 'nite-spot'. I have a sort of impatient soul filled with opprobrium at the mention of the word 'nite-spot'. A night-club is the nearest terrestrial invention to hell. A huge noise in a confined, smelly and smoky hole. A bottle of liquor that costs twenty times its otherwise over-the-counter price. Dim lights and the ridiculous pursuit of enjoyment. A headache and a foul mouth are the pointless consequences.

But Jenny comes from Beckenham, and she went to read English in Liverpool University, and down that street there is a small bar, with a hanging sign and a locked door with a little grilled port-hole, and this is 'Jenny's Place'.

So after supper, and at a time when sensible people would start to think about going to bed with their collected Lyttelton-Hart Davis letters, I set out for Jenny's Place.

She was dressed in the regulation black of night. Tight black of night. Ample of bosom and generous of thigh.

Mouth like a red rosebud and twinkling black eyes. It sounds like the middle verse of some traditional Irish song. She doesn't, however, sing Irish songs. She has the full international repertoire. Piaf blends into Garland, and that slides to the latest Bavarian smash-hit, and on into the night. The inside of Jenny's Place is rather like the old Bertorelli's in Queensway, just on the north side of Hyde Park. It's comfortable, and if you were being generous, you would describe it as 'well-used'. And if you were being honest, you would call it a little shabby.

The night I went, there was an equal mix of locals and visiting Europeans. The barman and the other girls speak or shout in German. There is a three-piece band. The drummer, Freddie, now aged, say, 75, short-sighted, dapper, drumming with his fingers on the table when his sticks are at rest, played for Goebbels in the earlier and more triumphant times of the Third Reich. Dr Goebbels was, as we know, in charge of propaganda, and made strenuous efforts to attack British minds, ears and imaginations by every possible channel. He ordered that popular songs of the day should have their lyrics reorganised. The words would be changed to express sentiments of mocking triumph. So that when unsuspecting little Englanders were tuning their wireless and searching out a station, they would come across a well-known tune with a new Nazi gloss upon it. And this Freddie, sitting next to me with his half glass of beer, kept the rhythm moving. There was no choice. Choice, I suspect, never entered his head. Why should it?

Did I expect him to have said, 'Ah well, Dr Goebbels, now I don't think this is exactly the sort of behaviour we Germans should be practising in the hours of our superiority. We shall only frighten and confuse our enemies, and there are some things to which even the art of the drummer should not stoop.'

He played. And he was paid for playing. And he didn't ask any awkward questions. It is not until the turmoil of that conflict has long subsided that the air becomes clear enough, empty enough, you might say, for the questing traveller to fill it with liberal speculation. It is, in other words, an indulgence. Did I expect Freddie to be ashamed? Well . . . I didn't expect him to appear almost proud of his activities. But then, I happen to be on the winning side. And, although nobody could hear us, we used to sit in the air-raid shelter in Saunders Road and sing about Hitler having only one ball . . . 'but poor old Goebbels had no balls at all'.

Meanwhile Jenny passed the table on her way to the little stage.

'What do you think of it all?'

'I'm lost,' I said, looking around.

'Don't be too unnerved. Think of this. Bavaria is the Yorkshire of Germany.' And she swanned off.

You can get lost in the topography of comparison. When people say, 'Well, of course, Morecambe is the Benidorm of Lancashire,' you have three disparate concepts to juggle across the atlas of the brain.

'What do you mean?' I shouted.

'Well, all the men have fat hairy knees and all the women make puddings!'

She was, in a manner of speaking, right.

I met another girl in Jenny's Place. She rejoices in the real name of Vera Calabria. Her father was, until recently, the Brazilian Ambassador to Western Germany. Here we go again with the dizzy geography of the shrinking world. Vera Calabria has settled down in Munich. She works, in all kinds of satisfyingly peripheral ways, in the theatre and the opera house. She speaks perfect English. She has a sharp eye for detail and an oblique and entirely personal sense of humour. She saw, in an instant, that I was behaving in rather a rudderless sort of way, and she offered to pick up the limp baton, for the next morning.

There is an old gate to the south side of the city of Munich. It is like a fort, heavy, substantial and forbidding. It contains a small mad house, and this is where Vera Calabria took me. Through a little door in the side wall, you enter a museum that is dedicated to the life and works of Karl Valentin.

'Who is he?' I asked, knowing Vera now well enough not to have to pretend to be a knowledgeable and accomplished traveller.

'Wait and see,' she replied, impishly, as we climbed a narrow winding stair.

He was born, I learned, at the end of the nineteenth century and died in 1948. He started his working life as a carpenter until he grew into the confidence of a humorous artist. He drew, and made sketches and designs for theatre sets. He started to work in film. Eventually he blossomed as a performer, and in that intoxicating time in Germany, between 1928 and 1935, became hugely popular. There is a statue of him in the Market Place. He has long, thin hands, and the statutory sad and distracted air of the great clown. He was obviously an intelligent and sensitive man. His pictures and his drawings have a satisfying sense of design, but they do not provide the lunatic focus of the museum.

A short list of his creations should indicate the fertility of Valentin's mind. 'A winter toothpick' stands in a little case. It is, of course, an ordinary toothpick but has a tiny fur bonnet, to keep the delicate thing warm during long cold hours of idleness. Next to that a special pair of corsets and brassière, designed to arrange the pouting breasts in a particularly fulsome way. Valentin's explanation, which I could only dimly understand, was something to do with engineering works to increase a normal milk yield.

The rarest item in the collection, and, according to the handbook, one of the rarest sights in the civilised world, is a small bottle containing the 'sweat of a civil servant'. There is a rejuvenating machine which has gone wrong. The subject of this rapid experiment in turning back time is mummified in a glass case. It looks like a girl doll except for the large black moustache on the upper lip.

A crowd of day trippers were wandering around this funhouse. They were making the same shrieks and guffaws that you hear on the Pleasure Beach at Blackpool. There was a particularly thoughtful group standing and staring at a tin tray containing maybe an inch of still water.

'What is it?'

'Well, you've missed it, really. It was a beautiful and delicate ice sculpture, but you're too late.'

'Would you like to come over here and see a basket of unlaid eggs?'

And, of course, being the simple traveller, and lost in a certain amount of wonder, and wandering in a foreign land,

and not properly understanding the language, and seeking to please, and to appear rather cosmopolitan, I followed the cheerful guide to examine the basket of unlaid eggs.

They looked pretty much like any other box of unlaid eggs, just not nestling there comfortably in their little box of straw.

★   ★   ★

At about this time, moving always away from England, and beginning to smell the South, I was suddenly confronted by the Church. Hit, in a way, by God, by a Divinity, by a mysterious encounter for which I was not properly prepared.

Hitherto, on the journey, I had not so much avoided the Church as been indifferent to it. I was raised in the rather washily moderate Church of England. Too much of this can blank out the mind, and dull any sense of wonder or excitement. Three times each Sunday – Communion at eight o'clock of a dark winter's morning was not a bright highway to salvation; Matins at half-past ten, and a long pointless sermon delivered by a vicar with small awareness of the power of theatrical thunder; Evensong at half-past six, sharing a cold church with worthy and dedicated worshippers most of whom were there because they had no one else to share anything with. There were no 'Excused Church' notes for me to brandish, since I was taken by my father, for whom only a death rattle would have been a possible consideration for absence.

Then, because of this constant limestone drip of exposure, I discovered one day, in late adolescence, that the King James Bible and Archbishop Cranmer's *Book of Common Prayer* combined what my influential English master called 'good stuff, meaty stuff, stuff with gristle and energy'. If he said that, or, because he said that, and because by now I knew much of it by heart, I grew less depressed by my visits.

Then I left home, and was translated to Oxford, and discovered there the glories of English Church Music. Every night of term, I walked from my own college, Exeter, across to New College Chapel, and sat, mystified in the half-light, to listen to the music.

I suppose that everything happened the right way round. Better to have had a hard ground drill in the language and the literature, and then to discover the glory and the beauty of architecture, painting, iconography, music. Whatever happened, anyway, happened by accident and circumstance.

In the now middle years, I can see virtue and sense in the disciplines of the Catholic Church. And if you add that to a constant need to belong to a society which, itself, is ruled and organised, then I am a likely candidate for conversion. As yet, of course, I am too green, too liberal and too unrepentant to take that thorny road.

God forbid that I should call my day at Chiemsee, with Sister Scholastica, any kind of lesson. But I came away wiser and by no means sadder. If you take the road south from Munich, you come to a scatter of attractive lakes set in low hills and pasturelands. It is a very popular playground for the rich of Munich who enjoy the peculiar pleasure of 'messing about in boats'. This, the largest of these lakes, is called Chiemsee, and I had never heard of it. In the middle of the waters, surrounded by trees, hidden from the shore, is a Benedictine Monastery. Locally, it is known as Frauen Chiemsee, the Dames Island.

I puttered over the placid lake in a little motor boat that occasionally developed a mind of its own. On the jetty, in long black robes and white wimple, stood Sister Scholastica. You know how, frequently, you develop a hard printed image simply from a given name? Scholastica, apart from being difficult to spell, pronounce, but not to remember, has a crisp teaching edge to it. It is a no-nonsense name. A name of some seriousness and high purpose.

As I tied up the boat and clambered out to say early hellos, I could detect a hint of accent and a twinkle behind steel-framed glasses. The accent is a mixture of Austrian, where she taught for 14 years, and Droylesden, Manchester, where she was born and spent her formative years. It's a strange mix.

It was a strange meeting.

We walked briskly to the monastery. There were crowds of visitors. This being a Benedictine house, there is a strong tradition of hospitality. Sister Scholastica is in charge of

Meeting Sister Scholastica, Chiemsee

those who come to stay, to contemplate, to enjoy, to forget. She took me through a throng of schoolchildren and souvenir hunters into the private garden. On the way, she greeted everybody. In the garden, she became pensive.

She has just made her first vows at Chiemsee. They bind her to this place for three years, and after those three years, she must make a final decision, as also must the community. If they both agree, and each accepts the other, it will be forever.

One of the vows, difficult to explain, she says, is called Conversazio Morum.

'The interpretation that I like is simply "Monastic Life". It means that I am willing, in every situation, to align myself to God's will for me. Every situation!'

'Without question?'

Pause. Gaze. Frown. Then back to the twinkling.

'I don't think you could ask anyone from Droylesden to do anything without question. But basically I have learned, from experience, and *not* from being taught, that God has the reins in his hands and I can leave it to him. If I give my life over to an authority, which I have, they see parts of me that I perhaps have not, or cannot, see myself. They can make more of me.'

'Do you like yourself more now that you've taken these preliminary vows?'

'I like myself now more than I did two years ago. Simply because I am more likeable than I was two years ago. I'm certainly gentler. Gentler with myself, and much more gentle with other people. And don't forget, you have to live here with 49 other individuals.'

'Have you made friends . . . or . . . enemies?'

'You don't need to *make* the enemies. They're here. If you allow them.'

'Love? Thoughts of love? Thoughts of the joys of the flesh, the body?'

'I most certainly have not lost the ability to feel emotions. None of us has. There isn't any kind of balsam that you can take to stop you from looking at somebody too closely, and breeding an emotion you can't automatically deal with. I've become, in a kind of way, more explosive since I came here. I have to talk to the Abbess about it. And I do. I get angry.'

We are at that point of the conversation where my instinct presses me to go on, to intrude, to ask for a specific instance of this kind of human trial. We are, at the same time, at that point where she indicates, not by any word or movement, that such a question would be insensitive.

'"Scholastica" is an intriguing name,' I say.

'We can choose our own names, but Scholastica seems to have chosen me. It means pupil, and St Benedict thinks' – it was interesting that she used the living present tense – 'of his monastery as being a school of the Lord's service. And what better position to have in the Lord's school than that of a pupil?

'School in Manchester was always a very great joy for me. I wasn't particularly bright. I went to school on my fifth birthday. It was a present for me. My mother, I suppose, was pleased to have me out of the house. But to me, school meant everything. I've had to do exams all my life. I had to do Austrian university qualifications and I did the finals two days before I entered here. Scholastica is not perhaps the least appropriate name for me.

'When you have served your novitiate, they – the sisters – vote for you with black and white beans. They pop the little beans into a box. Your future – maybe the rest of your life – rests upon a bean in a box. Except, of course, it doesn't. It rests with God.'

We are sitting together, still, in the garden. The previous

Abbess, now of advanced years, is sitting in the far corner, near a yellow rose tree, snoozing. It is quite another world. Without sounding too dainty, it is almost like being in a waiting-room for some gentle paradise.

'Here we are,' I venture, 'surrounded by water. Do you not feel trapped at all?'

'Well, you know, some young nuns feel trapped, and some of the pupils who come here to study think that they've landed in Alcatraz. But we're not really enclosed because we can go for walks on the island. And the island is beautiful. If we have to go away, for some special reason –'

'Like what?'

'Like going to the dentist . . . then we get a special blessing, and when we come back we get another special blessing. To welcome us back home, back into the family.'

It is a gentle, scented summer's day. Not, as it turns out, Sister Scholastica's favourite time of the year.

'I like winter best. Because there are not so many tourists. In summer, the ships can bring 700 tourists in an hour – 701 with you – and it only takes twenty minutes to walk round the whole island. But winter – in the early morning . . . We're allowed then to stroll the island walks, after breakfast, and – no joking – it is just like the dawn of creation. Beautiful. To take in the silence, and to let it live with us.'

I know quite well that, given another splash of technicolour and the soaringly sentimental strings of a Hollywood orchestra, we could easily be into a scene from *The Sound of Music*. It wasn't that way. It was warm, and revealing, with Droylesden and Alcatraz as points of extreme reference. And in this long, entertaining and sometimes exhausting journey, it offered the possibility of contemplation and, paradoxically, a sense of creeping deadly sin – envy. School, church, the disciplines of a routine, the calling toll of the bell, the structure of a society well-ordered, the certainty of the next day, winter, and the ultimate hope of salvation . . .

I left Sister Scholastica on the jetty. I said goodbye to her. She asked me to come back in less frenetic circumstances. She gave me a kiss. I felt honoured. I felt happy.

★　　★　　★

Bavaria is a place of confusions. Saintliness on the one hand, and madness on the other. They say that Hitler was mad, and this view was not held simply by my Granny Harty, lying in her bed, as the bombers droned overhead, spitting defiance at the Fuehrer. They, whoever they are, were right when the ultimate horrors of the gas chambers were half-shown to the world. Mad, in this context, means pouring out evil – insanity destroying everything in its crushing path.

But there is another kind of madness, which, by accident, I fell upon in this part of my journey. I had looked at the travel guides and the posters issued by those whose job it is to persuade visitors to come here. They all, at some time, draw attention to the presence of Mad King Ludwig. So far, that was a name, a figure of recent history, a date, something of a character, but in no real way enigmatic. Just 'Mad King'. Visconti had made a film of the same name. The 'hero' was played by a swashbuckling Bavarian, a film star eventually translated to the more sanitised madness of *Dallas*, or *Dynasty* – who remembers which? – whose name was Helmut Berger.

It was, of course, Ludwig who built the castle at Neuschwanstein, with its fairyland towers et cetera, and its grand dramatic emplacement on the top of a high rocky outcrop, surrounded by steep woods and washed with waterfalls which drop from such a height that the cascade seems almost frozen in its descent.

The castle is used in practically every poster. And it's an advertiser's dream. As a mise-en-scène, it is unbeatable. Given a certain suspension of disbelief and a fat film budget, anything is possible. A man could swing across a ravine with a box of chocolates. A man could swing across the ravine advertising a particularly delicate brand of monkey nut. It's the sort of place where the Mayor of Carmine could win a war – any war. In the shops nearby you can buy misty photographs turned into postcards, which have obviously been washed into unreality.

When you get there, up a long and winding road, it is disappointing. Ludwig's money ran out. More precisely, the coffers of the Bavarian government had been so rigorously raided by the King that, after one or two secret crisis meetings, his ministers decided to put an end to this profligacy. They put an end to him as well.

It was my misfortune to see the castle of Neuschwanstein on a clear and sunny day. No frost to sharpen the outline. No mist to shroud the surrounding plain and allow this structure to float on its necessary cloud. The sad truth is that, from the approaching road, it looks like a power station. And because it has clean upstanding towers, it looks, more precisely, like a *nuclear* power station. The nearer you get, the more lumpen it appears. Outside, therefore, it failed to live up to its handsome promise. In fairness, one ought to say that there are many such places, scattered through this European journey, which provided similar disappointment. A promise unfulfilled.

Inside, it looks like a rambling version of Keble College, Oxford, with the addition of some of the public rooms of the Randolph Hotel in the same city – before it had electric light dimmers, fitted carpets, and the inevitability of a distant microwave in the model kitchen. It is, entirely, not to my taste. Heavy, gloomy, brassy, indulgent, with a state bed so isolated and uninviting that it looks like Ayers Rock on a flat Monday. Stairs and steps, everywhere, to turrets and towers and corridors. There is a cumbersome ballroom and an unfinished throne-room. If you have been to the little church that stands next to its exquisite campanile on the island of Torcello, in the Venetian lagoon, and if you have stood at the back and looked at the High Altar, and if you then – in this stretching exercise – could close your eyes and imagine what all that early medieval simplicity would look like if you had hired the services of a tasteless and extravagant interior designer to 'do it up', then you would open your eyes and see this throneless room. Attractive or impressive it certainly is not. The only redeeming features of this architectural exercise are the views from the high windows. And poor Ludwig spent only one hundred and seventy-two days here – in what a sane person would call his prison.

However, should you go back in time to Ludwig's earlier days and a castle which he commissioned at a time of his life more rounded in its enthusiasms, less troubled in its dreams, you will arrive at Linderhof – hidden in the depths of a wooden valley, an hour's drive from Neuschwanstein. Imagine some capricious God suddenly extending his magic finger and pointing it, say, at Chatsworth in Derbyshire, casting a particular spell that would shrink its palatial dimensions, and then lift it gently away like a fragile decorated cake and set it down, icing intact, in Bavaria. That is Linderhof.

It lies in the hollow of its private, watered valley. It is ornate, fussy, small, white, and very beautiful. I am not given in any way to over-decoration, to the baroque. Nor, for that matter, am I given to playing football, or climbing Everest. But when I can see clearly the confidence – arrogance almost – with which Hillary sticks his flag into a summit, and the coolness of Bryan Robson who sees the right moment and the right place for a strike at goal, then I know that I am witness to some achievement beyond my individual scope.

If you stand at the front of this particular palace, a toy, a plaything almost, you look out upon a small rectangular lake with a high and splashy fountain sweeping up the waters, then handing them slowly back to the basin. If you stand at the foot of Ludwig's bed and look out of the window, you see a long, high staircase, a series of step-stones, down which flows the water from the mountainside before it disappears underground to be received, eventually, into the turmoil of the fountain in the front courtyard. And over this moving water, there is a house of domestic proportions, where, for some part of his short life, I presume Ludwig, Mad King Ludwig of Bavaria, had time to enjoy himself.

He was a passionate man, and being King, decided that he may as well behave like one. Some Kings yearn for anonymity. Some ride bicycles through their less capital streets. Others prefer to get away from the drone of their court and breathe the Highland air; shoot and fish and walk the favourite dog. Occasionally, a monarch grows intoxicated with his power and privilege, and topples into the conviction that he is not necessarily God's representative on earth, but that, rather, God may be his representative in heaven. Then heads roll, innocents are put away, horses are made consuls, favours are bestowed, bribes generously – and dangerously – received; and when fate's grisly hounds bark finally at the

The Mad King of Bavaria

panelled door, all that is left is a vast store-room containing three thousand pairs of shoes, and a jotted list of private Swiss bank accounts. Then it is time for the people to burn your picture, and evacuate on your statue . . . or do I mean, piss in your sink?

I am now quite convinced that Ludwig was misunderstood and I do not want any historian with access to hitherto unpublished accounts of diaries to upset my conviction. It is quite possible for a man to be born out of his time, and out of his own circumstance. No contemporary seemed to understand Ludwig's passion and admiration for Wagner, for instance, whom he befriended and encouraged, with warm exclamations of enthusiasm, and with a great deal of money. He's patently mad, they said. But who now would question his munificence? Parenthetically, Wagner does not exactly come out of this relationship, if such it may be called, smelling of lilies. There is a fawning and a festering somewhere inside it all.

In my private portrait of this, as yet, Mad King, I have also perceived a kind of shyness. He was inordinately fond of the theatre and, in particular, of the opera. But when he travelled to Munich, the State capital, he occupied a Royal box that gave him full view of the stage, but hid his presence totally from the audience. There were no gracious waves, no bowing acceptance of ritualistic applause. No acknowledgement of the claque. His presence was virtually a secret.

One large part of Ludwig's life was arid, empty, unfulfilled. He was not the marrying kind. He preferred the company of men, and young and handsome men at that. He was not, in any sense, greenery-yallery, niminy-piminy. He was restless enough to hunt, shoot, explore, climb even – but perhaps not every mountain. However, there was no one to share the private moments, no one to dissect the pleasures and boredoms of the past, no one to applaud a secret act of generosity, or to criticise or prevent an indulgence like Neuschwanstein. It is not a peculiar or unique or even rare situation that he endured. And it is certainly not made clear, by any existing record, whether this isolation sprang from his regal position, or from a vicious mole of nature.

Whatever the reason, one may be certain that those who

worked for him and were, in various places, able to call themselves neighbours, conceived an admiration and an affection for him. In the gripping loneliness of an evening's solitude, he would, all of a sudden, order that his carriage, or in winter his sledge be made ready for a night ride. You can imagine the response from the servants, with their skate boots off, toes roasting round a fire, doors locked, horses stabled, dogs yawning, when they suddenly heard the alarum call the excursion.

'He's off again. Where to this time? You go tonight. I went last night.'

That is the downstairs side. Upstairs, who knows what he wanted or where he would go? On these lonely journeys through lanes, farmlands and forests, he would order the carriage to stop at any cotter's light. It is recorded that he was made welcome – invariably. It is, in fairness, hardly likely that the door would be slammed in his face, followed by a rude oath telling him to get back home. There are endless speculative possibilities of a Python nature in these chance calls.

'Come in. Come in. Wipe your feet. Cold night, isn't it. How are you feeling then? (Pause) I'll just tell Hildegard you've come. (Pause) Guess who's just come, Hildegard. It's King Ludwig. KING LUD . . . Never mind, she's a bit deaf, our Hildegard. Take off your fur coat. Nice bit of stuff. How are you then? Put your feet on the fender. Well, Ludwig, you must be mad – mad! – to come out on a night like this. We were just saying, they're getting on quite nicely with Neuschwanstein. Aren't they, King Ludwig?'

But if, on the frosty morrow, it was Hildegard's birthday, or a wedding, or a funeral, Ludwig would make a small note to remind himself to send a gift, a present. Not a Fabergé egg. What would Hildegard do with a Fabergé egg? Except dust it. No. Something substantial but acceptable. Bottles of wine, a haunch of venison: he was, in a sense, a capriciously random Father Christmas.

Then time ran out – because money had run out. If you are that lonely and that unloved, except as a person of position, then emotional insurance costs rather more than the crust and the water which sustains true love in an attic.

It was time, the government decreed, to put an end to the increasingly manic grandeur of the King's behaviour. They didn't send troops because they knew that those who lived with him and near him would die for him, and – since the situation was difficult enough as it stood – the last thing they wanted was a whiff of persecutory scandal. Instead, they sent doctors, who would certify him. Then they could be rid of their prodigal sovereign, by clean and clinical extraction. The health of the State could be restored, and someone with a little more sense and a little less vision, could then occupy the throne.

The learned doctors, consequently, notebooks in hand, made their way to Neuschwanstein. There was a difficult moment at the gates, when the villagers, hearing of their arrival, and of their lord's imminent disposal, decided to bar their entrance. They called out the fire brigade, who willingly mounted a defending guard and threatened to blow the medicine men off the mountainside with their water cannon. But sense – reason, right, might? – sense prevailed. King Ludwig bade them welcome, either because he was mad, or because he was a gentleman. Or, perhaps, because he was both.

Secret plans were laid to spirit him away, to convey him to a 'quiet house'. But he had developed a curious friendship with Dr von Gudden. Ludwig knew that he was a prisoner. He knew that his movements were closely watched, and recorded. Dr von Gudden fell into the habit of requesting a walk with him, through the estate, in the early evening. Even in those days, a breath of fresh air was well-considered to be restorative, if not 'damned right improving'.

On the last night of his life, Ludwig set out before supper to walk to the lakeside with the doctor. He had not returned by eight o'clock. They found his body floating, upwards, in shallow water, some two hours later. The doctor was not far away. Both bodies were brought back to the castle. There was no sign of a struggle, no marks, no clues.

This, as you see, is the stuff that films are made of. Visconti plunged into the dramatic waters and nominated Helmut Berger to fill the complex and tragic rôle of Ludwig. In a moment's temporary confusion, I hit upon the idea that Mr

Berger, who lives near to the scenes of his former dramatic triumphs, would be the ideal guide. He, after all, dressed in Ludwig's capacious furs, slept in his bed, rode out on a winter's night in the fantastically carved Royal sledge, dined at the King's table, and would, no doubt, have a thousand private insights into the emotional mechanisms of this disturbing shadow.

Now I am wise, as ever, after the event. And sadder. If there is such a thing as personal chemistry, then an analyst would be able to detect traces of gunpowder and poison in the chemistry created by our meeting. Normally, in situations of such difficulty, when clearly I am not at ease, not 'getting on', as they say – not even getting through, as it happened – I would weigh all of the blame on myself. I am the one having the 'off' day, surely. I am being wholly unreasonable in asking Herr Berger about Ludwig's loneliness, his supposed madness – of course I am.

We sat, uncomfortably, on the edge of the little lake, in front of the Palace of Linderhof. We sat side by side on a stone parapet. I may as well have been calling, on a very bad line, from some outer satellite of Saturn. He was petulant, he was suspicious. I said that I thought the Palace of Linderhof, arranged like an exquisitely decorated ice-cake in an emerald forest, was a surprise to me: it was so small, so intimate. That was an observation. He confirmed that I was wrong, and that any pop star had a pad like that in Hollywood, and what was I supposed to be saying?

'Asking, really,' I said – or asked.

'My nose is hurting,' was the next response.

This was the first time in my Grand Tour that I wanted the San Andreas fault to forsake its subterranean fury in western California, and to snake out to southern Germany and swallow either him or me. But, dear God of Earthquakes, not both of us. *Not* together. I was in such a deep and difficult hole already. How should I climb out with any shred of dignity? Let alone enjoyment.

Here is perhaps the most vivid, the most complex, the grandest European character I would encounter on this journey. So much more intriguing than Wellington. More dashing than Nureyev. More secretive and much more naive than Mrs Castle. And here is a man, a man who must, for his daily bread, speak other men's lines, and who for six months long was Ludwig, slept even in the same Royal bed, wore his furs, rode secretly in his secret sledge, dined at his table . . . Am I being insensitive in asking for a small light by which to half-illuminate so large a personality?

'Where is the make-up lady?' asked Mr Berger. 'I have coughed.'

★   ★   ★

At the back of Linderhof, cut out of the hillside, is a large grotto. It was fashionable in the earlier part of the nineteenth century to decorate a garden with reminders of antiquity. Ludwig ordered the manufacture of a large underground cavern – modelled upon the Emperor Tiberius's fun palace in Capri. Visconti, in his film, directed a scene of orgiastic suggestion on the lake in this grotto. But by the time we reached this secret place, relations were as cold and inhospitable as the prevailing damp atmosphere. For a long moment, I began to lose my protective enthusiasm for Ludwig. Maybe there was something in this particular part of Bavaria, even perhaps especially in the grounds of Linderhof, that made grown men mad.

The grotto is, by anyone's standards, overpowering. There is a lake in this Stygian cave upon which sits forlorn a large boat, shaped like a scallop shell, with a sail and oars. It is going and has gone nowhere. It is frozen in the dramatic and isolated aspic of a man's dream. The theatricality of this underground folly is emphasised by the large backdrop of a painted curtain, depicting a scene from *Tannhauser*. The place is discreetly floodlit. The colour of the lights changes to reflect the mood. Angry blue, an inflammation of red, an envious green. In one kind of fanciful way the traffic lights of a Dream King's unnatural highway.

Near to my home in Yorkshire, there is a worthy band of volunteers who constitute the Cave Rescue Organisation. They help people who, by lack of planning or – more usually – by a sudden shift of the weather, find themselves in the depths of difficulty. There was never a man in more need of their assistance than I was on that day. Herr Berger knew the escape route, literally and metaphorically. I was trapped.

When eventually I found my way out into the warm air, I felt so angry I wanted to kick something, a rock, a wall, a statue, myself. Either that, or plunge into the cooling and healing stream of alcohol. I did not kick anything. But, two hours later, I felt a lot better, thank you.

'My wardrobe,' said Mr Berger, sadly, 'it is déshabillé.'

Up until my encounter with Helmut Berger I had thought that the principle of the baton, passed from one generous runner to the next, had worked reasonably well. Fatiguing for them, maybe. Enjoyable and enlightening for me. But the rôle of the baton is essentially a passive one. Herr Berger had, to my mind, got hold of the wrong end of the stick. He was using this useful device as a cane to beat me with.

In the colder light of a Northern day, way back home, recollected in somewhat agitated tranquillity, I am happy to say that Herr Helmut Berger did not put King Ludwig out of favour. Rather he added yet another layer of complexity. I have scratched about the myth and read more about the Mad King since. I am still unable to tell a hawk from a handsaw, no matter which way the wind is blowing.

I reckon that I am entitled to my opinion as much as the psychiatrist, the fire brigade, the historian or the actor. I know, in my marrow, that Ludwig's generosity, which is embodied in Linderhof, gradually became inflamed through isolation, and then caught fire and burned itself into a different shape, contorted itself into the grotesque and unfinished pile at Neuschwanstein. And at the fire's height, he put himself out by an horrifically simple immersion in still, shallow water.

In this bleak humour, I escaped to Oberammergau, a place of a different kind of pilgrimage. Friends warned me. They had been to the Passion Play some years before. Their chief impression had been one of acute discomfort, their backsides significantly branded, on account of the hard wooden seating, into the shape of a cross. Friends had warned me about Oberammergau.

★   ★   ★

I left Germany by way of Unterammergau, the lesser known

of these neighbouring towns – the one that is regularly over-shadowed, the understudy – where I stopped for a good beer and a liberal think.

The conclusions, as ever, were unexpected and complicated. As soon as I may, I shall return to Germany – to the south, especially. I was astonished by the grandeur and the space. I felt at home with puddings and dumplings and chaste lace curtains, doorsteps polished to a reflection. Maybe it's the passing of time. Everything changes, and, most particularly, so do I. I am now a European. The enemy can no longer be a German in a helmet with a swastika on his armband. The enemy is ignorance. And in this part of my journey, I have been confronted by new things, ideas, vistas, have learned from them, have seen new sights; have transformed an old prejudice into a new preference. Even, perhaps, grown up a little.

If ever I needed confirmation of purpose – a reason, not an excuse – to travel, I have it here, at the end of my first full Grand Tour of the hitherto foreign and unexplored lands of Germany.

CHAPTER
FIVE

In the Bible, which is not, with Michelin and Lyttelton-Hart Davis, a part of my luggage, it says, 'In my end is my beginning!' And that is churning quite frighteningly through my mind as I lie on a hot slab in Evian, at the end of my grand journey through Switzerland.

I left you, or you left me, whichever, sorting out Germany, leaving Unterammergau, and of a disturbed disposition. See me now as I prepare to leave Switzerland, the next leg, forced to lie on a hard bed in the Royal Club in Evian. Apart from the ever-flowing waters, I have subscribed to a necessary health regime. I am due to arrive, shortly, in Italy. I strongly believe that this is where I am heading and that, somehow, a natural force called gravity or personal inclination will deliver me energetically to the South – the ultimate goal of all Grand Tourists, to a place where I may, satisfyingly, clip my wings and settle in a reflective nest.

Meanwhile, what with one thing and another, I need purging. There have been hiccups of late. Too strong a personal diet. There are always the odd indigestible lumps between wherever is here and there. And it is more difficult, and more irritating, to have a break down in relationships than to suffer some mechanical failure which an expert, or even an apprentice, can quickly mend. That having been said, someone is now hard at work upon my body, on the slab. I think she is trying to put a brave face on me. I came in this morning, across the water of the beautiful Lake Geneva, full of good cheer, infected by the bonhomie and the generosity of Peter Ustinov who entertained me at his modest house on the opposite shore. No sooner had I set foot on land than I was overtaken by the improving machinery of the Health Club. Track suit, which made me look odd – or odder. A fulsome and windswept girl of athletic proportions, the sort of girl who has been chipped out of menthol-fresh ice, the kind whose face has never been visited by a passing spot, an upright-seeming girl who has, I think, yet to have her first hangover.

She is there to improve by challenge. She gives you a series of directed instructions and makes sure you complete them. Her hardest task is not to laugh. Mine is not to despair. This, of course, appeals again to the Protestant ethic. It is the underlying philosophy of syrup of figs. It tastes like hell which is why it's doing you good. Eat up, drink up and be not too merry, in case it happens tomorrow.

I have already run twice round the estate. The second time, it took me twice as long to cover the same distance. You are not given time to recover breath or composure. Dotted through the wooded grounds, there are service stations. I thought they were resting places but they are points at which you stretch and bend, and do this with your arms, and do that with your back. It all sounds frightfully jolly and, presumably, if you were sharing the experience with a lot of jolly fat people from Garstang, you could make it one long breathless laugh.

At one point, you are confronted by a lot of logs placed side by side to make a kind of raft. You have, with feet and ankles together, to spring over it from a standing start. When you finally achieve this preposterous goal, on the thirty-seventh leap, Irmgard or Ingrid (something harsh and uncompromising like that), pushes you onwards, and instead of throwing you whatever is the equivalent of a dog biscuit, as a reward, she delivers you to the Archers. Then, there are a lot of funny jokes about being put through hell in order to meet the Archers (exact identity not specified –

could be Ambridge, could be Grantchester), and these little quips would perhaps be tolerably amusing if you had any part of your panting frame you could divert to the service of humour.

The Archer could not see the point of any of the accompanying laughter. He looked at his watch, and looked at the sun, and looked at me, and I had no idea what message he was seeking to convey. I suppose that those who choose the staff of these intensive health farms have a clear image of the kind of staff they want. This gentleman looked like a competent air-steward, on a day off. You would, perhaps, put your life in his hands in some kind of extreme emergency. But not a gentleman in whom you would wish to confide your little weaknesses.

If I had not been so exhausted, I think I might have enjoyed my session with the bow and arrow. Sometimes, even still, I surprise myself with a hitherto untested capability. Three years ago, I took my family to the Pleasure Beach at Blackpool. When I was tired of being whizzed around in gravity-defying machines for £1.50 (VAT included), I stopped at a shooting range. They gave me a rifle. I aimed at various tin cans and astonished those who were with me by so accurate an aim. I can also play the organ, and the piano; and I am a good car driver, and this list surprises others as, sometimes, it surprises me. I took hold of the large bow and plucked a light aluminium arrow from my quiver. The Archer gave me a sort of glove which prevents the firing arrow from burning the skin from your fingers. His instructions were precise, clipped and unequivocal. Left arm out at a right angle to the body and held stiff. String brought fully back by right hand. Aim taken by looking at centre of target – one thousand miles away – through fixed sight on bow. The strength required to keep all the machinery steady is formidable. To begin with I had bow and arrow wobbling in such a palsy that the spectators were stepping smartly outside the widest of angles. I took eventual steady aim and let the arrow sing its way to the target. It hit the next ring from the bull's eye. There was a ripple of startled approval, and I felt my stature increase by the size of one cubit. Suddenly, the morning's training had produced an unexpected result. Look!

There is the missile embedded in its target. Show me the nearest chamois hunt, point me towards a wild boar, give me Hiawatha's clothes, play the overture from William Tell!

Before I could become too arrogant in the acquisition of this new skill, there was more stuffing to knock out of me. My blond guide bade me lay my weapons aside, and run again, behind her. She brought me to the rooms I now inhabit. She shook my hand, thanked me for my efforts, almost clicked her heels and was away.

Ladies in white coats, behaving like sanitised tugs, then nudged the liner of my body into a private mooring. Here was I, full of the joys of archery, seeking confirmation of my sporting prowess. But I had done with all that.

'Go into that room and take off your clothes.'

'I beg your pardon!'

'Please, be not ashamed. Take off clothes and get into bath. I will come to you later.'

Now, when you are out an-archering, you know more or less what is expected. Here is a bow, there is an arrow, that is the target. But in this 'Salon d'Esthétique' there were no rules, and no book, and no list of regulations.

If I take off my clothes, should I lock the door? If I lock the door, how will she get in? What will she do when she is here anyway? There is, indeed, a bath. Quite a large one. The bottom is not flat but slightly moulded to the contours of a semi-sitting position. There are too many taps. They have strange names on them. There is already a bathful of water.

No sooner had I settled myself in the bath in rather an ungainly posture than the door was flung back and the wardress strode in with a bottle. I covered those parts which ordinary wardresses do not reach. She seemed unconcerned and emptied the contents of the bottle into the water, wrenched all the taps and wiped her hands, and said she would be back in half an hour. Meanwhile, the great turbines under the surface of this now green liquid began to churn and turn. Once the body had accommodated itself to each fresh attack, and, bear in mind, these came from unexpected and subaqueous corners, then a mesmerising rhythm began to rock one, to and fro, so that a sleep was soon settling gently upon the tired frame.

I was jolted from a distant reverie, having dreamed of being a successful archer, by the eruption of the white lady, who arrived to turn off the taps.

'What should I do now?'

'Put gown on and follow me.'

I wrapped myself in the white robes of the other acolytes of the Health Club and peeped out of the door.

'Go there,' she said, pointing to a white door.

'Everything here is white,' I said to the new caretaker.

'Sit down,' she said. She put a towel round my neck and asked me to draw the chair up to a table which contained various bottles. In the middle of the table and attached to the wall was an instrument, like a small fat gun, or a hairdryer.

'Make sure you sit in front of it directly,' she said.

'How do I know if it will go off?' I asked, in a half-jokey manner. But there were to be no jokes here, thank you.

'It *will* go off. Keep your eyes closed.' Those two sentences contain contradictory intelligences. If it is going to go off, whatever *it* is, then I should have my eyes open in order to avoid it. Shouldn't I? I placed myself in the twisting hands of the white witch and waited. There was a hissing sound. Then a gurgling.

'It is water which sprays a face to clean.'

There was a cold but not unpleasant sting to the first outburst. Thereafter it became a gentle, satisfying rinse. I relaxed, calming myself with the knowledge that all this would be quietly transforming my lined and fatigued face. She came to turn off the spray and to dab me with towels, white towels.

'Do I seem to be much more handsome?' again misreading the charts.

'This water is from Evian. Not from Lourdes!'

Dab. Dab. Dab. And then I was taken to this slab, upon which I am still resting and remembering. Before I tell you what I remember of my journey through the land of chocolates (good), cuckoo clocks (not so good), and bank accounts (very good) called Switzerland, let me tell you of my physical circumstance.

The latest wardress, who has just left this white cell, I have only seen upside down. That is, she has been standing behind me, so that I have squinted at an unrecognisable collection of features. She, no doubt, has the same view of me. She is giving me a new face. She has been at it for nearly an hour. I watched her, out of the eyes that are in the back of my head, mixing a heavy (white) paste. Then, having positioned me, as if I were a body to be mummified, she took a trowel and began to lay the paste upon my upturned face.

I asked her if she had ever read a poem by Philip Larkin, the verse in which he describes a stonily indifferent Plantaganet knight atop his tomb. She shook her head and placed one finger upon her lips to sign me to be silent. She is probably still wondering who Philip Larkin is and whether she's ever had him plastered. The sensation of plaster thickening and hardening around the face is not unpleasant to begin with. Then it is. Two things were unexpected. She started to cover over my mouth, and signed me to start to breathe through my nose. This caused me to become afraid – sensations of drowning and sweating rose up in me. The heat thus generated from my hot face was reflected and contained within the plaster casement, and my head felt as though, suddenly, it was on fire.

She signed for me to keep perfectly still. And she never told me when she would come back and release me from my beautifying bond. That was a quarter of an hour ago. The clock faces me, and the hands of time, which have hitherto circled like the clocks of a fast cartoon, have now slowed down.

I am not moving. But thinking. Me and Stevie Smith. Drifting back. It isn't so hot. I am sleepy.

Switzerland, then, began in Zürich. Frank Delaney, no mean traveller, was passing, by accident, from the monastic rocks of the Skelligs, off the West Coast of Ireland, through Europe, and on to Constantinople, tracing the steps of an Irish monk of the Dark Ages, on his way to the Holy Land. As a part of his research, Delaney was visiting the University Library in Zürich. But our meeting was almost entirely concerned with the influence of this city upon others. In particular, the fact that Zürich was a comfortable and unexpected harbour for James Joyce. Now, apart from the customary stab at *Ulysses*, and the constant strains of hero worship whenever I am in Dublin, I knew little about the nearly blind, thin, waspish Irish giant.

Delaney, in a congenial café, with a handy drink, took out his word sketch book and made several lightning pages of entertainment for me.

'He loved this city, you know. He particularly enjoyed berating the citizens for having forgotten the virtue of filth. See how clean and organised Zürich is. Even the perceptive Mrs Woolf, Virginia, I mean ('Yes. Frank.') said, "Oh that Mr Joyce, he's nothing but a boot boy picking at his pimples".'

When you looked out of the window of our café, the Odéon, all you could see were large leaden buildings, tramcars clanking heavily along the street's length, banks, offices, and people moving purposefully, but not swiftly or lightly, upon their business errands. Hardly, I would have thought, a place for someone of James Joyce's fizz and fancy to find creatively genial.

'Ah, well now! He disliked war. He disliked violence. He disliked politics. He disliked religion. He disliked all the conventional things that populate normal towns. Well, now, Switzerland was neutral, and here, in Zürich, it was cold and clinical, and rather like, I suppose, a scientist puts a culture that he's developing into a fridge, so Joyce must have seen himself putting his own imagination into the fridge that is Zürich, and letting it grow, and flourish.'

This is the kind of moment to cherish on a tour. Any tour. A small tour, a grand tour or a détour. I simply love sitting in comfort and being warmed by the enthusiasm of a good storyteller. There are plenty of atavistic precedents. And if you can't find easy access to the literary tradition, then make good use of the oral.

'I like this place,' I said, indicating the zinc bar and the busy waiters who look like waiters, wearing over-long white aprons and balancing their trays upon carefully outstretched palms.

'You're right, lad,' said Mr Delaney. 'So did Joyce. Used to sit over there and drink a dry white wine. Drank enormous quantities of it. He wasn't supposed to drink, you know. Had glaucoma, badly, which caused him awful pain.

'They used to sit near the lavatories, look, there. And he would arrange to meet his wife Nora here, but he would somehow get hold of an extra bottle of the stuff, and shove it inside his jacket. And she was fond of the beer, which is why they sat there. And every time she went out to spend a penny, he would take huge swigs of the stuff. By the end of a pleasant evening, of course, he was in a very happy mood. And when they were walking home, Nora used to say how marvellous it was to see him on such good form without, indeed, any drink taken!'

As this pleasant morning progresses, I can see Joyce beginning to materialise in our midst.

'He was on his way,' says Delaney, on *his* way again, 'on his way here, to this café, one day, with an English painter called Frank Budgen.

'"What have you done today?" asked Budgen, and Joyce replied, "I had a marvellous day. I spent the entire day, uninterrupted, working on Ulysses." "Did you get much done?" asked Budgen. "I did. I did. I completed two entire sentences!"'

Then, when we had tumbled through Joyce, and Nora, and Frank Budgen and all the Irish crowd, we took a tramcar into the suburbs, to see the sights or such sights as there were. A wet Sunday afternoon in Zürich must be a time when one's resistance to the pressures of drabness and provincialism is at its lowest ebb. But this was not a wet Sunday. It was a cool and showery Thursday, late in the morning. Mr Delaney wore the suit of a jaunty Irish traveller and carried a large furled umbrella. Nobody talked on the tramcar. Nobody smiled. The conductor stared at the driver's head, and the driver stared at the tramlines, and we rambled on.

'Look. You can see why he liked it. Because it's suitably dull, suitably neutral. The buildings are extremely boring, and the women look bored. There is nothing here to arrest the senses. There is no impediment to the imagination, so that it can float absolutely free. Joyce had a blank canvas. If he'd been living in Dublin, he'd never have been able to write. There's too much going on there. Too many excitements. This place is boring enough to produce great art, and great thought. Freud was here, you know. So was Jung. The

Dadaists sprang into energetic life here. Let's get off the train, and go to the cemetery. That'll be less boring.'

Frank Delaney had never seen the grave of his literary hero, nor the statue erected by the people of Zürich in his honour. That wasn't boring of them, was it?

'Buried here in 1941. January. Statue erected later, but look at it. Thick, heavy glasses. His sight was so appalling that he went out to buy a second-hand white jacket from a dentist, so that, when he sat in the window, some of the light would reflect off the white jacket.

'This statue . . . never seen it for real before . . . it has two qualities. It captures the thin spidery quality – he used to do a little spider dance – a caper. And then, it captures the seedy elegance of a man who was described as a marsh fowl, watching everybody. Or, as James Stephens called him, "a tall, blind, beautiful man".'

We wandered up and down the cemetery. Formal alleys. Clipped short box hedges. A small legion of gardeners taking out plants that were almost dead and filling the spaces with trays full of blooms. No litter and, even more extraordinary, all the litter bins empty. Do the workmen take the bits and pieces home? Or is the citizenry so well trained that they stuff their sweet papers in their pockets?

The brief but entertaining pilgrimage in search of James Joyce was now completed. We came back down on the tram, past the house Joyce rented. It is now a psychiatric clinic, with his name upon it. Still, that says little about Joyce, or the clinic, or even Zürich. They make Brontë Biscuits near Haworth in Yorkshire. And there is a Coleridge Café outside Grasmere. So no deep significance can be read into the change and rededication of the dwelling of a genius.

On the way back to town we chatted about the trials and triumphs of travel, about chance encounters, about the importance of a hotel bedroom and, eventually, to the question of one's own behaviour in a strange land. The Grand Tourist, the one in the frock coat and a tricorne hat who would stand in a romantic attitude and gaze, at some length, at a mountain or a palace, must have possessed that most valuable of commodities called 'time'. There seems in all contemporary accounts no urgency, no sudden desire to drop all and run back. In truth, many of the travellers were the younger sons of aristocratic fathers. To be despatched to the continent of Europe in order to observe, at first hand, how other nations lived, worked and played seemed then to be a suitable way of killing two birds with one cultural stone. The young man could, at the same time, afford the experience of leisure. He was rarely examined when he returned. And, if too closely questioned, would have by that time been schooled in the smooth practice of deceit. Some travellers were, in effect, sent upon errands of duplicity. They were spies. Look at the lazy and foppish behaviour of the Scarlet Pimpernel. Here is another English milord, who will be drunk with our strong foreign brew by the time night falls. We need not cloak the exchange of information. He is too foolish to know. Talk on. Except that, sometimes, the English milord had an ear that was too cocky for close examination. And an eye too bright.

If, however, I stop, as I do now with Mr Delaney to examine the purpose of my journey and the progress of it so far, I reach for different conclusions.

The purpose is that of enlightenment and entertainment. I have travelled much more frequently since I was sprung out of a weekly television studio. Once of a day, I believed that the mountain would come to Mohammed, but the next day it didn't, and I had to go and look for it. And I fell then into the habit of moving. Since I have always, at the deepest possible root, been a schoolteacher, I like to tell people stories, to show them things, to share my enthusiasms, and occasionally need to confirm my prejudices. The purpose isn't any more significant than that. Huw Wheldon, whom I respected and loved, told me, again and again, 'Just get them to sit down and then tell them a story.' He hit the nerve that all good teachers sometimes lose, and should, at all times, remember. In my first job, when very tough and adolescent lads were hurling furniture around the classroom and swearing at each other, and at me, as though they were at home, I made damn sure that I got into the stories as quickly as I could. That, and a little of the blinding pepper of sarcasm which, unfortunately, I have never been able to avoid, and I kept myself afloat.

Here is what Frank Delaney has been offering to me in Zürich. He sat me down and taught me. Told me stories about Joyce. Stories I am passing on because they intrigue me and I hope, in turn, that they will interest other people.

But the late twentieth century is a speedier time, and this journey is not being undertaken in the relaxed aspic of the eighteenth century. There is time to stand and stare, but the time is strictly limited.

In the middle of a stand, or at the end of a stare, it is quite likely that a telephone will ring. I am not the second son of a Lord. I am the first son of a fruiterer who couldn't understand decimal currency, and suffered because of it. So I earn my living by telling stories to other people. Showing them things they might not otherwise see. And showing them through the dangerous filter of my own vision. On my passport, next to the word 'Occupation', there reads the word 'Broadcaster' and that is, strictly speaking, an offence against the Trades Descriptions Act. It should, more accurately, read 'Narrowcaster'. When I travel, or work, or broadcast, or talk, I know that I am never going to stand, fixed, forever, under a Niagara of unqualified praise. I used to think that in earlier days when, at the same time, I thought of myself as God's newly created gift to the business of communication. All that or, more honestly, some of all that, has changed. I am no longer unsifted in such perilous circumstance. So that when the telephone rings, I want to answer it. It may be someone in a position of power or privilege calling to say that they quite like the idea of a 'Grand Tour' and maybe I should make notes of preparation about it. It is not my job to eschew the twentieth century and live in a cultivated limbo.

That is why the bedside light switch needs to work. That is why I must carry an electric adaptor in my night bag. Together with two tooth brushes and a clothes peg. The peg was given to me by my mother when she sold that same family house in which the French Étienne stayed. She took down the washing line in the backyard and gave me the one peg left dangling. It has been a travelling talisman since that saddish day. Things don't go brilliantly right when I carry it about but they don't go sadly wrong. I did not, for instance, have it about my person on the day I was arrested in Siena.

That, however, is another tale.

In a modern sort of way, I regard my stock of Red Michelins as talismen. The problem is, of course, that not only must you change them at the border, but at the year's end, too. A rosette can quickly fade and die, and a man cannot live off the smell of yesterday's mashed potatoes. Who will now extol the virtues of ancienne cuisine?

In the Swiss edition of the Michelin, there is a healthy recommendation of a restaurant called The Kronenhalle. Delaney hadn't heard of it. I thought that a reasonable 'thank you' for his pains and his efforts – which didn't seem to me too much of a painful effort – would be a wholesome Zürich dinner, possibly to continue our conversation. Possibly to gossip about colleagues. Explore the faithfulness or falsity of friends.

Oddly enough, The Kronenhalle is next door but two to The Odéon where I had my first brush with Joyce. The façade of this restaurant is vastly undistinguished, supposing, that is, that there are degrees of undistinction. It could be a warehouse, or a block of flats, or anything that is located in the centre of Zürich. Let us now dispose of the restaurant. It's so good that it does not need me to underline its Michelin entry. So often, in my travels, I have found no need to quarrel with my Michelin. So. The food is good. The wine is properly presented. The waiters are civil. This chair is comfortable. The view is pleasant. But, you ask, where is the 'but'? But, I've done it, I've seen it, and I don't want to go back, to repeat it. Something is missing. When I look round The Kronenhalle I wonder what it can be. With the exception to which I shall eventually devote myself, it looks like a busy night at the Connaught Grill. That is to say, there is a lot of polished wood. But then, not everyone is wearing a jacket or a tie. And there are no precisely ranked knives and forks, flanking a white plate which will be removed before the first course is served. If you look to your right, you will see two gnomes, two big gnomes, crunching fresh bread, baked in the house, crumbs scattered around the white cloth. These crumbs become counters, coins, abacuses or abaci, squadrons, stocks, shares. They are moved this way and that. They become the currency, albeit in flour and water, of a bitter financial debate. Or, they are the means of avoiding a direct proposition between this hungry man and that desirable woman.

See him, with his finger on a large piece, delicately manoeuvre the point of his proposal so that it slides seductively to her smaller part. Maybe, in the magic of numbers, embarked upon in a Parisian café, it will be the seventh crumb which sets the seal. There is a vigorous precedent for a seventh seal. It may be heresy to say that women make better waiters than men. In which case I need to invoke the protection of personal preference. I was served, for many a glorious Friday night, by Anna at Bertorelli's in Queensway. She set the standard. It was perhaps an accident that she was born a woman. She didn't become a very good waitress by accident. That was design. And the Kronenhalle is well served by waitresses. There are waiters, too. They seem less obvious.

Remember that I am searching here for some rare quality that does not appear in guide books. Woodwork, casual clothes, bits of bread and waitresses. That could, of course, be a Little Chef.

I had better come clean. I know what the answer is, and I know that there isn't room in Michelin to offer this kind of diagnosis. There may not even be an inclination. The answer is that this house is ruled, benignly, by a dynastic force called Zumsteg. The present holder of this proud Zürich name is Alfred Zumsteg. He looks like a suave version of Sir Ian McGregor. He has that same quiet almost lethal reserve. He watches you. He waits. His mother was the basic inspiration. She started her working life with 50 centimes. She spent ten of them on the same day. She worked in a private house as a servant. Then she married Sir Alfred's step-father and they opened this restaurant in Zürich. The father, the real one, is not mentioned. There are hazy parallels with Catherine Cookson. Here we are dealing with dedicated, zealous, ambitious achievers. Mrs Zumsteg whipped up the restaurant to its current splendour. Alfred, her son, took charge of the decorations.

How many restaurants, on the winding trail of this Grand Tour, could you enter without making a prior booking, and be conducted to a table, over there, against the wall, to sit under an original Matisse? Maybe the other table is more favoured. They, all four of them, are sitting underneath a vast and gloriously blue Chagall. Two of them have their unseeing backs to the splendour and are less favoured. But they can feast upon a Picasso, to their right.

Suddenly, Zürich is not boring any more. What have I stumbled across? What wealth, what discernment, what apparently carefree approach to the world's most fashionably measured artists? There is (and this does not appear in my Michelin) no protective cover over any of these pictures. Yes, maybe there is the odd accident. Like an over-happy diner who took his knife to another Chagall and, in an irritable moment, carved a hole in it. But that happens rarely. The diners, according to Mr Zumsteg, are, on the whole, well-behaved and appreciative.

If this place were simply an acquisitor's palace, I don't think I would have been taken to the private apartment where there is more of the same, only, if you see what I mean, different. In the seclusion of the sitting-room Alfred Zumsteg quietly, almost nonchalantly, reveals the sources of this passion. He began to collect those things he liked. He abhors the word 'investment'. A lot of my curiosity is powered by commerce. What kind of fortune lines these walls? Is this private collection, which is, I have to say, the most impressive private collection I have seen, able to be insured? The questions are either irrelevant or, even worse, obtrusive.

'I have had to make every franc myself. To earn it all myself. Even borrow the money, some more to pay the debt. It was always a sacrifice. But when I love the painting – and I love all of these. I mean love. Love. Then the sacrifice is worth it. Once I had so much debt, I had to sell four paintings at once, and that hurted (sic) me. It will hurt me to the end of my life.

'I am sad that anybody regards art as an investment, which it has become. Because people who really love it cannot afford it any more.'

I had visions of the restaurant, downstairs, at one point in its earlier life, as a place full of talent and artistic energy.

'Yes. Chagall came to eat. Miró. And Léger. Francis Bacon comes. Henry Moore enjoyed his visits, or so he said.'

'Do you ever change the hangings of the pictures in the restaurant, like you change the menu?'

The response takes a time in coming.

'Sometimes. You have to be careful. The customers, old and valued customers, come here because they recognise the ambience and they like it. Sometimes the change aids the digestion.'

We came back, inevitably, to James Joyce. Yes. He had his regular table but, more interestingly, when he died Zumsteg's mother secretly supported Nora Barnacle (Mrs Joyce). She still appeared almost every night to supper. There was, then, little or no money and the bill was discreetly removed so that the question of payment never arose. It was a mutually agreeable arrangement. There is a small charcoal drawing of Joyce in the corner near Mrs Joyce's usual table.

There is a twist, a silken twist, to the end of this tale. Alfred Zumsteg, sitting in splendour but also in the anonymity of Zürich, is not a restaurateur. Others look after that side of the well-organised house. He is a manufacturer of silks. Rare ones. Now, it is not all that long ago since I was sitting in an equally unpretentious apartment in Lyon with the Brochier brothers. Autre pays, but the same mœurs.

'The great choice of my life, and I made this choice consciously, was to become a silk manufacturer and designer. I had the opportunity, at one point, to become an art dealer. And I tell you this without any pretence, or any pretentiousness, I would have been one of the greatest art dealers of this century. I had all the contacts. I knew everybody. I knew every painter. And I didn't follow that because I did not want to mix my love and my work. I loved them. I didn't want to be commercial with them. I was sitting on the edge of the bed of Matisse; he was a little paralysed and making a collage. I helped him. I had some pins. I said put the pins here, and here. I had personal friends. These were friends . . . not my business. I can make business with silk, but not friends.'

★   ★   ★

Recommendation is a strong propelling feature of this enter-

prise. 'When you're in so-and-so, you must take time out to
go just a few miles down the road to see . . . whatever it is.'
So that, when it came time to take leave of Zürich, I had
pricked down Einsiedeln for the next stop. Just before we
leave this ponderous Swiss city, however, let me say that
here is another instance in which a pre-conception is first
crystallised into a conception, and then, by an accident of
nature, fractured and re-formed. Boring old Zürich, with its
heavy buildings and lumps of lead on wheels called trams,
and people with their heads looking down to the clean pavements. Boring old conservative Zürich, where I heard
Anthony Burgess say that a man had been arrested in the
street at midnight by the police. For what? For laughing!
Grey Zürich. Clinical Zürich. Financial Zürich. And all
these characteristics remain evident. But Delaney has
planted the idea of a selective prison – a place whose service
provides perfect freedom. And Alfred Zumsteg, bidding me
a gracious farewell, told me never to judge a book by its
cover. In this chastened mood, I followed the recommendation to Einsiedeln. There are, as it happens, other people
who know about other places and I should not in this progress lightly disregard them.

I had no guide book. Just a map. I had no image. No pre-
conception. Nothing with which to chip at the concrete
pediment of a reputation. When you start to pick up signs for
the comfortable Swiss town, you find yourself driving
through a high undulating landscape. There isn't an Alp in
sight – but the air is cold and clear. And the chalets could be
shrunk by a magician and arranged tastefully upon the
shelves of a souvenir shop. There are flowers in rolled green
carpets. And there is a most enviable and orderly stack of
arranged logs – winter fuel – placed against the outer wall of
the houses. Then you swing into the centre of Einsiedeln
and, in the middle of the town, is a large basin or bowl where
visitors collect. It isn't a square or a piazza. It is a re-filling
small reservoir of coaches and travellers and taxis and buses.
It is dominated by the huge façade of an abbey. With twin
towers, and fancy stone-work, and an air of wealthy preservation. When I had parked the car and wandered to the
central door of this huge ecclesiastical pile, I was surrounded

by groups of farmers and their wives clearly dressed for an occasion. The snob comes to the surface again as I attempt to describe their appearance. They may not have been farmers. They may have been gnomes out from the heavylands of Zürich, disguised as farmers for reasons of security. Whoever they were, they seemed to be enjoying the wedding of one's son and another's daughter. They were farmers because the gentlemen's suits were black and tight and shiny, and all the buttons were fastened. The women wore strange hats and dresses that seemed to have been sewn from a pattern book. And, the snobbiest observation of them all, they had hired the services of a video cameraman to record the happy day. They disappeared into the glorious church in no particular order and without any formality. Then they were bombarded by one of the most inspiring and enlarging sounds of the European church.

Einsiedeln is the last Swiss home of the Gregorian chant. If you pin down a resident priest (Benedictine, again!) he will tell you that this is, maybe, the finest Gregorian choir in Europe. Then, in more expansive mood, the *only* Gregorian chanters in Europe and, as the music soars up to the clerestory, the only practitioners of this rare and dying art in the world. 'What about some of the places in France?' I ventured. 'Places like the great Abbey at Solesmes?' There is a thunderous silence. The priest looks not so much through me as through the back wall, five hundred yards away. This is the big ecclesiastical brush-off.

Then they sang for me. It was a private performance, in the small chapel behind the high altar. I sat in a big stall on one side with my eyes closed. They stood opposite, each man in his particular stall. They had their arms folded under their black cassocks. They had no conductor, except a kind of leader who stood, paradoxically, behind them. They chanted an Easter Office. They thereby sealed time, froze that moment, as an unexpected, expensive almost priceless gift from a band of brothers to a passing tourist.

When I make more than a brief reference to being a privileged traveller, I am thinking of precise moments like this. Again, thoughts of such a crazy mixture and confusion occupied me in the closed-eyed reverie. This is where I want to live for the rest of my life. Forsaking all others. Dedicated band. A timetable. No push and shove. No store set by acquisition. No competition. Except . . . 'We do it with more gracefulness and more, how do you say, manliness. We are not so precious.'

You see they are competing. But competing isn't so bad if, like Daley Thompson, you get used to occupying the winning position.

'Will you sing something else for me?' I boldly asked the senior father.

'No, thank you, the brothers will now go to supper. Goodbye. Please come back.'

It does a man's heart good to know, in a depressingly Protestant way, that he cannot have everything he wants. That was my Gregorian ration. Take it, I did willingly. Who would leave it? So, with humming and singing, and with all the conscious uplift of another encounter with Saint Benedict, I started up the engines for another direction, another turn.

Tomorrow I must spend the day in Liechtenstein. In the morning I have to go to the world's biggest false teeth factory. Are they the world's biggest false teeth, or is it the factory that is the world's biggest? In the afternoon I shall climb the hill, the little mountain, to the Royal castle of Vaduz to meet Prince Hans-Adam, the heir apparent to this principality.

The postage stamps and the tough businessmen I had

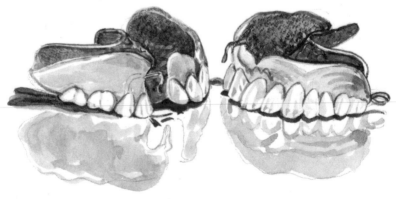

Liechtenstein

heard of. The false teeth, if you will forgive me for saying so, were an eye-opener. It will come as no surprise when I say that I have never devoted a great deal of time to wondering how and when these essential auxiliaries are made. I once took my father's upper set, in a brown paper bag, to a dentist called Mr Lord, in Northgate, and I remember him putting them on a circular pedestal and walking around this mildly offensive and deeply personal object, muttering to himself.

'Where's the tooth, then?' he asked.

'Er . . . it's in the apple,' I replied shortly.

'And where, pray, is the apple?'

'It's in the fire.'

And so progressed this little exercise into the Pinterland of personal hygiene. When Mr Lord had stopped muttering he said it wouldn't be a cheap job, oh, dear me, no. I said I thought we could afford it, thank you, and could I have the paper bag back?

The things I learned in the Tooth Factory in Liechtenstein are interesting but not, I imagine, useful. Except for any passing teeth fanatics who are into a little light industrial espionage.

The raw material is quartz ground into powder, with oil, water and lanolin added to make a paste. (This is starting to sound like a food programme.) There is a magical menu card. You look at pictures of teeth, and then say, 'I'll have three of those and two each of those,' and so on.

Germans buy more than any other nation.

Australians want them unnaturally white. Italians, God bless them, are not particularly concerned one way or another. The English, wouldn't you know, don't want to talk about them. The French prefer them sharp-ish. Here are the roots of fantasy, which no one will decently explore with me. Netherlanders want them flat! Greeks prefer unglazed plates, so that they can throw them around in restaurants. Laplanders need a fur lining. Tyroleans need space to whistle through. Swiss want gold fillings and a secret reference number. No questions asked.

I didn't take any photographs on the trip. I am allergic to cameras – he said, travelling with two cameramen and a brigade of engineers – and I tend to avoid groups of enthusiasts who have expensive equipment strung around their necks, and little bags with F2 9 ZERO BALTEX zoom equalisers, and little machines that flicker in the sunlight and tell you about the width of your shutter and the length of your exposure. They, again, are the secret builders of the Forth Bridge in matches. They make the Crystal Palace out of used yoghurt cartons. You will know who I mean, unless you are such a one as these. Then you won't. The same group, I fear, call evening meetings upon their return from the Himalayas or the Grand Canyon and have slide shows in their sitting-rooms. 'Wait till we draw the curtains. Wait until the machine warms up. How has that hair got through the transparency and across the Tower of Pisa?'

What need of a camera if you can rely upon the blank retina of your imagination? Images, hard, crisp, coloured pictures, stick to this. A box of quails' eggs, untouched. A box of eggs, unlaid. Carp's semen on toast. A pair of false teeth. And these I can (tastefully) arrange upon the personal canvas I carry in my mind. My canvas has, of course, the advantage of expanding sides. Into this canvas now strides the tall and youthfully paternalistic figure of Prince Hans-Adam, the Heir-Apparent to the tiny but influential crown of Liechtenstein. He is the first hi-tech Prince I have met. He looks like the prosperous businessman that he is. The fingers of the Royal hand are upon the financial pulses of Hong Kong, Tokyo, Paris, London and New York. This castle of Vaduz may be the merest fly-speck on the European route I travel, but it has all the small-packed power of a micro-chip. Swift, accurate, lean.

'My children teach me how to use the computer.' It takes a small leap of the imagination to re-draw the lines of established and wealthy aristocracy from a long traditional entrenched position in a medieval fort to a twentieth-century businessman in a busy office. Here is ticker-tape and the distinctly unmedieval smell of new electrical machinery, even though in one corner is a heavy decorated wooden lectern of the sixteenth century. Sometimes this tall Prince tots up the odd figure standing at this reading desk. It helps the posture and reminds him of his past.

The diffidence of this businessman springs, in part, from

the low profile of the family, and part from new intrusions since the house and the hills became a place for the Prince and Princess of Wales to take the odd ski-ing holiday. Newspapers, he says, now want to know what you eat for breakfast, what you do at home at night, whether, indeed, you are human.

This castle, as Duncan rather misguidedly said of another place, has a pleasant seat. The air is sweet and nimble. And there are no signs of reconstruction or offensive repair. That is not to say that the whole place is of an architectural piece. It is in higgledy-piggledy harmony with the landscape. There's a covered bridge across the deep slit of a protective ravine. There's an open drawbridge, and further inside a huge iron grill of a gate that opens by electric eye, and clangs loudly behind you as you have passed through. So that, if you did penetrate this fastness for any malicious purpose, you would find it almost impossible to get away.

The family belongs firmly in that impossible entanglement of Austrian and Czech dynasties, marrying, enlarging estates, warring, collecting, but having no profound influence upon European events. The names are too numerous to list, and their arms need a microscope to read.

'My father,' says the Prince, 'named me Hans-Adam after one of his predecessors who was very successful in business, in acquisition, in the hope that I would be successful too. Up to now luckily that has proved quite correct.'

There are those who say that the Swiss work too hard, the Austrians play too hard but the Liechtensteiners have just about got it right. He says he agrees, but mainly because they know when it's time to go to sleep.

There is no apparent border between Switzerland and Liechtenstein. The scenery does not change. The mountains are grand, the valleys flat and the cows all look like each other anyway. The streets are clean. Wealth is evident. What, then, is there for a Prince of such a family to worry about? There is a chink in the easy composure.

'We always have to worry, especially a small country which cannot defend itself. We worry that we can keep peace and freedom in this part of the world so that we can survive as we have done in the past. We had a time in the Second

World War when we were close to being taken by the Third Reich, occupied, that is. And there were times before that when we did not know whether we could survive. We've managed up to now. All we could do is pour boiling oil out of the window.'

If anything were poured over these battlements, it would fall upon a small art gallery down in the main street of Vaduz. There, the family collection is on public display. A part of it, that is. Their inventories, which they found holed up in the cellars, along with preserved pictures, date the start of the collection well back to the middle of the sixteenth century. No one bothered too much. There was no curator. No keeper of the Royal pictures. Some were sold in hardish times. Others bought by whim. Hans-Adam calls it an 'Up and Down' collection.

What is now down, physically, is worth two and a half Kings' ransoms. Huge, rich, round, ripe Rubens. Not exactly to my taste. If you were to manoeuvre four of them into a rectangle, you could provide yourself with the walls of a substantial house, with interior decorations of the very highest order. It may be a kind of artistic heresy to say that I find Rubens too large for comfort. If you were able to step into his pictures, you would feel as though you were wining and dining with gods the size of moored barrage balloons. Eye-level is nearly always thigh level. Everything is flab and fat. (Flab and fat are the enemies at this moment, since, you will recall, I am lying like a bound Lazarus slimmed down in the Health Club in Evian. Peter Paul Rubens is a fearsome threat to my drifting dreams.)

In the corner of the main hall of the gallery are two small Breughels. 'Small' is here a relative term. One of them is a picture of *The Census at Bethlehem*. The other depicts a parable of *The Blind Leading the Blind*. Breathtaking. Simple. The paint almost in primary colours. The composition full of the business of everyday life. It is, in effect, Breughel's back yard into which wander the smallest Mary with a little bundle of Jesus and a weary Joseph with his bag of tools. The rest of the world (or the village) is unaware of the momentous arrival. Children fight. Youths skate. Men and women are busy in the exchange and marketing of cheese and wine.

Fires warm old hands.

I stood for a long time looking at this exquisite picture. The other, *The Blind Leading the Blind*, seems cruel by comparison. The ways are stoney, and one man must cling, almost viciously, to another in order to avoid the pitfalls of the unstated journey. As a metaphor it made me uncomfortable in what, after all, is almost the mid-point of a Grand Tour.

CHAPTER
SIX

O scar Wilde said that the Alps were objects of appallingly bad taste. He would, wouldn't he. Howsoever, they are not to be ignored. They do place an awful constraint upon a traveller wishing to describe them. If they are simply the highest places in all Europe, with what do you compare them? It is both pointless and diminishing to tell someone to imagine Helvellyn, and then multiply it by ten, twenty, thirty. It doesn't mean anything. But with a combination of ingenuity and precision the Swiss have made quite sure that they, the Alps, that is, are not merely dramatic backcloths to the domestic activities of a town in a valley. Roads zig-zag to the summit. Engineers have made masterful mechanical conquest of high peaks. Railways crawl into clouds. Restaurants slowly revolve, in the bright sun, above them.

This morning I woke early. By appointment. This is the morning, in the little village of Appenzell, that the farmers and their cowherds had marked off in the year's diary as the day upon which they would undertake their annual cattle run. It all sounds rather like the distant thunder of hooves in Marlboro' Country. It is, thank God, much less macho than that. These cowboys, as I suppose you may rightfully call them, wear embroidered waistcoats and black hats, three-quarter length trousers and white socks, and look like they are on their way to rehearse a chorus from *Hansel and Gretel*. In other words, they are in regulation Swiss national costume. There are no women; if there were they would be in dirndls. They are at home, making rosti and hanging their duvets out of the bedroom window.

When I say early, I mean very early. It is half-past four o'clock, and it is a dark morning. The mist is down to knee level. There is a drizzle. It is very silent in the heart of the town. Then, from a distance, comes the sound of a tinny bell, and then another. And the volume increases into a gentle jangle. The cows are coming!

They are on the move from their winter stables, and the shelter of the valleys, up to the high pastures. It is a ritual journey. The cows do not seem too enthusiastic. They mooch along the street, sniffing at closed shop doorways, and attempting to turn left into the churchyard and call it a day. The cowherds are more resolute and make whooping noises. There are children with sticks to beat the kine. But they seem disinclined to exercise such harsh behaviour; and the procession moves onwards and out into the meadows, and the cows sniff a fresher air. Once they are on their way and the climb has begun, the cowboys develop a thirst. At six o'clock, with one in shivering tow, they are passing their first inn. Outside, the landlord and his wife have prepared a small table, with glasses. When the landlord hears the bells coming up the road, he opens a bottle of wine. The cowboys run from the back of the herd, take large swigs, wipe their mouths with the back of their horny hands and then set off to catch the cattle who are now moving of their own determined volition. The trouble is that there is another inn two hundred yards along the road where the same ritual must be observed. Then another. The cows, somehow, have now developed the speed and appearance of frightened greyhounds. The cowboys are, to put it mildly, deliriously happy even though it's only twenty-past seven. Their dogs seem confused. Should they snap at the advancing herds or cower by their jolly masters. They can't be in two places at the same time.

All that is left, at eight o'clock as the sun bursts out over

To summer pasture. Appenzell. Switzerland

the top of a jagged Alp, is a flapping check tablecloth, empty glasses, the ordinary deposits of well-fed cows, gathered to garnish the garden roses, and me, in the middle of the road, listening to the fading bells, fondly imagining for all of thirty seconds that what I want to be more than anything in the world, more than a Prince or a chef or an Ambassador, is a simple farmer, on his way to summer fields in the mountains. It is as though I had just been playing a part in a commercial for cheese and milk and chocolate. A wholesome advertisement for things Swiss. Like all commercials, brief, vivid, very much to the point and more romantic than realistic. These cowboys have to live in sheds on high peaks. A lot of them don't have running water except for the fresh spring outside. They only see their wives on a Friday, when the women arrive with fresh stocks of food, and the dogs go mad. Otherwise, they are alone with the trolls and the whispering of angry giants, and the fury of the wind, and no video. They say that the cows come down with much greater enthusiasm than they've gone up. And the men do not even have time to pick up the return drinks. Maybe the grass is not always greener.

By half-past nine, I began to feel unusually healthy, keen even, to enjoy the ozone. A walk perhaps? A gentle promenade upon the lower slopes. Maybe a cup of hot chocolate somewhere in a convenient resting place. My companions that morning did not view this energetic prospect with any enthusiasm. At this stage, I did not smell a rat. That was partly because the smell of cow was all-pervasive, and partly because I had not yet understood that they had laid a trap.

'We'll take you for a cup of hot chocolate, but we can't walk to this place. It's too far. Get into the car.'

'No. No. Let's walk. It's a fine morning. It will make us feel better. We already feel virtuous, being up before the lark, or cuckoo. Let's walk.'

'No.' And that was that.

The car climbed through the wild flowers of the lower slopes and then stopped, nowhere. A huge man materialised from the meadow. His two large hands guided two large horses of Trojan proportions. He lifted me on to one of them and sprang lightly upon the other. This had all been arranged without my knowledge. I have only once been on a horse before, to try to learn the basics of the equestrian arts, when I was 14 and my sister was a natural mistress of the beast and wanted company when she went out to ride. My horse seemed to be interested in train-spotting. There was a bridge over the railway line near home. It had a low parapet. Lads would try to drop pennies into the funnels of engines. My horse, that first and last morning, smelt smoke and galloped to the parapet, and slithered to a four-hoof stop. And I continued up its neck, clinging and sweating, and fearing that I was to be pitched in front of a roaring train. I never went near horses again.

I didn't have much choice here in Switzerland. There was a little matter of pride at stake. Imagine the greater depth of fear when I discovered that there were no reins. One had to hold the saddle and go with. I complained a lot and swore a terrible revenge upon these stupid plotters. But my guide appeared unaware of any irregularity, and we headed, slowly and rather majestically, up into the mountains. Maybe there was something in the morning air – some essence of a proper communion with nature. I know it sounds highly unlikely, and I would never confess to enjoying it, but after, say, ten minutes, I felt a settling of the muscles at the back and a growing confidence, and I stopped shaking and shouting, and I looked to the left and the right, and whichever God inhabits those high lands nodded his approval, and we plodded on. A fine end to an eventful morning. I bade farewell to my Swiss Dobbin and, for a few heady moments, found the seat of the car hard and inhuman, and the view infinitely more circumscribed.

★   ★   ★

The journey to the top of the Jungfrau takes an hour and a half in a rack and pinion railway train. Half the time you have to hold on to the seat in front. If you put a bag on the floor, you will see it suddenly slide to the back of the carriage. You leave the scented valleys and their Lindt box flowers and climb through thick forests, and then thin forests, and finally above the permanent snow line. The train turns round corners to make the climb easier, so that, at one moment, you are looking down to the speck of a village and the next you are facing the flat north wall of the Eiger. Then it is you wonder how on earth, or almost in mid-heaven, anyone could cling to that death rock, let alone climb it. What drives men into the madness of mountaineering?

When you think the journey is never going to end, you slide into a tunnel, and the rock is very close to the window. This is not a recommended way for a claustrophobe to travel. Suddenly the train, horizontal by now, draws into a perfectly ordinary-looking platform. You have reached the top of the world. There are telephones and bookstalls and hamburgers, and all the necessities of a commercial traveller. It cannot be long before Benetton and The Body Shop open their doors in this vast supermarket in the sky.

They were doing a whacking good trade that day. You could see nothing from the enclosed observation platforms, but you could hear particles of ice and snow attacking the windows. And a forest of aerials, servicing one system or another, bent like bamboo in a typhoon. So everybody bought postcards and telephoned their families in Tokyo.

I have never seen so many Japanese. They have as much right to be infesting the top of the Jungfrau as I have but they were everywhere. In swarms. Little Japanese ladies pattered about in unsuitable high-heeled shoes or sandals with cold toes poking out. This year's regulation Japanese headwear is a floppy straw hat, decorated with flowers around the crown, a little battered, definitely from a superior hat stand in a country home. The sort of hat that Vita Sackville-West used to wear in the garden at Sissinghurst, when she rested, and saw that what she had created was good.

Beyond the coffee shop is the entrance to an ice-palace, carved out of the rocks of the summit, burrowing under the cone of the mountain. If you can bear the cold, you need to hold on to the walls, otherwise you fall over on the ice. I don't remember much of this white hell except for the screams of falling Japanese women. First one went down, dragging her friend behind her; then two more fell on top of them. It was like living in a mad ice-house. The husbands did what all husbands are expected to do in such an emergency. They photographed fallen women. From their nearly inscrutable faces, they seemed to be either wincing or laughing or, perhaps, both. The principles of oriental pleasure and occidental pain often produce the same facial contortion.

Restored to earth, back in a tea room in Interlaken, trying to thaw the hands and brain, I fell into conversation with Mr and Mrs Cobb, a retired English couple, feeling at home with a freshly brewed pot of tea, a plate of fancies and an impassive pianist tinkling out selections from *Bless the Bride*.

'This is the first time we've stayed in Switzerland for two weeks,' she says.

'Is that too long?' I ask, chewing a chocolate marzipan.

'Well. It is, and it isn't,' she answers diplomatically.

'It is,' he says, unequivocally.

'We're going on the train to Berne, tomorrow. There are plenty of shops and they have arcades so we won't get wet.'

It had rained every day of their holiday. They were fed up. There isn't much to do in Interlaken. There is plenty to see. On a clear crisp morning, you can see the Eiger, and the Jungfrau. On a clear, crisp afternoon, you can still see the Jungfrau and the Eiger and, if you cup you hand to your ear, you may be able to detect the sounds of Japanese women toppling over.

'There are a lot of Japanese here,' I said to Mrs Cobb.

'Crowds of them. I said to my husband only yesterday. I said I think that one of the ways they have of getting rid of unemployment is to send them all here.' And she laughed.

'And when they get to the top, they commit . . . what is that thing? . . . hari kari. So they send a fresh lot up!'

'There was one of them in the hotel and we felt sorry for her because, you see, she had one of those modern sophisticated suitcases with an electronic lock, and you open it with a plastic card. Well, of course, she'd lost the plastic card, and she couldn't get at her things. So I managed to force it open. Poor thing. She'd have had to go up the mountain in her skirt and blouse . . .'

'Like the rest of them?'

'Anyway,' said Mrs Cobb, ignoring this ignorant interjection. 'She was so grateful, she gave him all her toffees. Tokens of gratitude you might call them.'

I said I was surprised to discover that, apart from the

Japanese invasion, Interlaken felt so much like an English town. Here was everybody taking tea and pottering along the main street.

'There's nothing else to do. And the prices certainly are not English, I'll tell you. The reason why you don't see many English in here, having afternoon tea, is that they can't afford it. What *they* do is to go into a supermarket and buy tea bags and a flask, and some bread rolls and bits of ham, and sit on the railway station, like we did yesterday. What are you doing here, anyway?'

Again, I couldn't say I'm doing a Grand Tour. Not if they were going back to the station, even though they were on their way to Berne.

There are certain English people who can afford the Swiss prices. They tend to cling together in the fashionable resort of Gstaad. There is no smell in Gstaad. At least Interlaken has a busy station and the wettish smell of the watered tourists, and a few shops with fruit and flowers standing in the street. And Appenzell smelt of cows and all that goes with them or, more precisely, all that they leave behind. Gstaad has no smell. It is as though it had been placed behind glass and permanently cleansed, like Moyses Stevens' windows. The shops, rich shops. Cartier, St Laurent, Givenchy, Tissot, seem to be standing in an arcade that will eventually lead you to a tabernacular bank. Film stars, opera singers and Lear-jetsetters buy houses here. Whether they make their houses into homes I would not know. It was raining in Gstaad, as it had rained in Interlaken. Early summer and bitterly cold. Nobody in the streets, except one mad dog running backwards and forwards at a frenetic speed, complaining at the lack of action.

Where does Elizabeth Taylor live? Where is Roger Moore's house? Which is Julie Andrews' place? Sophia Loren? Joan Collins? The list is endless. Do they go to visit each other with albums of snapshots from their latest movies? Do they dine together, in the candlelit glow of a winter's night? Do artificial logs splutter in their expensive grates?

There were no answers to these, the fundamental questions which the modern Grand Tourist must ask. No one was in town.

The only place that showed any sign of life was the central dry cleaners. People were sidling in with plastic bags and striding out with neatly packed boxes. I saw a substantial-looking woman behind the counter. In another imaginary landscape she could well have been managing twelve looms in a Lancashire weaving shed. Or leading a team of naughty brownies into a woodland camp. She was a no-nonsense lady. She would know as much about this place as anybody.

She spoke little English, but we managed. She reeled off an indiscreet list of her likes and dislikes. She knows them all. You know how the London taxi driver talks at you through his driving mirror. He's the one who's had them all in the back of his cab, just where you are sitting now. Such-and-such is a real lady. Smells like a perfumed garden. Big tips. So, when you get out, either as a lady or a gentleman, you are forced to give a big tip in case you are villified by this judge of human nature when his next passenger settles into your seat.

This laundry lady let fly. Mrs Edwards is the favourite around these parts. That is Mrs Blake Edwards, whose maiden name is Julie Andrews. She is a real lady. She has no airs and graces. She has no 'snobisme'. She takes the children to school or to the shops. She drives the car. She comes in here with the laundry.

'Does she give you a quick burst of Edelweiss?'

'Certainly not.'

'Is Roger Moore the sort of unofficial mayor of Gstaad?' This information I had gathered in the bar the night before.

'He is a gentleman. Not more. Not less.'

We rehearsed a list of other international celebrities, their likes and dislikes, their manners, their moods.

'Elizabeth Taylor?'

She made a grunting noise. It grew louder. I felt as though I had just pulled the bottom brick out of the Aswan High Dam. A torrent of disapproval followed.

'She come in here, throw things in here, and she says "Wash this." "Do that."' Etc.

The etc. is mine. It stops the end of that particular sentence with an inclination towards propriety. I had to leave the shop because the windows were steaming up.

From Gstaad I telephoned Peter Ustinov to confirm our meeting, to remind him, in case he needed reminding, that I would call upon him after lunch, on the next day, and en route for Evian and the plastered rest I am now taking.

I went via Lausanne, to try an experiment. So much of my time has been spent, so far, in good hotels and bad, in quiet hotels and noisy, in expensive palaces and cheap rooms. The hotel is central to this whole venture. Most of my hand-books, recounting the details of the original travellers, tell of frightful nights in flea pits. Robbers bursting through rickety doors and relieving the alarmed guest of their money and their jewellery. Sometimes their clothes and, occasionally, their honour. The place where you lay your head at the end of a day's exhaustion, be it in contentment or dejection, can have a powerful effect upon your view of the place. I didn't, you will remember, care all that much for Belgium, but I loved Die Swaene in Bruges. And my comfortable rest house in Liechtenstein, with a Boots picture view from the big window, put me into a warm and receptive mood for the false teeth factory and the hi-tech Prince. We may make jokes about clocks, banks and chocolate, but the Swiss know how to accommodate a passing guest. The English are learning.

In Lausanne, there is a renowned École Hotelier. Students travel from all parts of Europe in order to learn some of the arts and most of the skills of the hotel business. It is such a tricky trade. Basically it is about a human being, and a bed. But then so is a hospital. Beyond the basic, it is to do with the needs of a traveller and how you can satisfy them corporately (as in 'Potage du Jour') or individually, as in 'poached egg on Bovril toast', the favourite dish of the Prime Minister when she and Mr Thatcher have a quiet night at home.

There are no grants to help you slide through the École in Lausanne. It's an expensive place. It looks like any modern European factory. Clean, low, big windows, coloured brick, ready-made shrubbery. You half expect a romantically sited schloss, with turrets and flags, and a footman to open the car door. But it is not like that.

Inside you could be in any polytechnic, except for the smell of something being flambéed. A student wanders along a corridor with a tray of clinking glasses. Four young women stand at a corner with note-books, making reference notes about 'the psychology of arrival'. The chance visitor starts to behave as though he were, maybe, in a hotel.

So much of this trade is to do with acting. I remember Jacques Tati suddenly springing out of his seat in a studio with me one day, to illustrate how quickly a cringing waiter could become an avenging gryphon. It had to do with a non-existent but nearly visible swing door – the door that led from the posh dining-room into the hell of the hotel kitchens. It was consummate mime but founded, obviously, on a truth.

Without too much difficulty, I persuaded the lecturer in charge to let me join the fun and games. The game is that I pretend to be a visitor, newly arrived at the hotel. There is a guinea pig of a student chosen to act as receptionist and another to carry the non-bags. The receptionist stands behind a desk which has nothing attached to it. He has to mime his dealings with me. It is all terribly serious. I begin to grow more outrageous in my demands. Does the shower work? Is there a mixer on the taps? The student will clearly go far. His answers are pleasant, firm, acceptable. He is not to be rattled, until I ask about the bells.

'What about the bells?' I asked haughtily.

'Bells?' he looked at me with a quizzical smile.

'What bells would they be, sir?'

'Bells. Bells . . .'

'Ah, bells . . . service bells?'

'Church bells,' I bellowed.

'They, sir, are on the side of the hotel, and they do not ring after midnight.'

I couldn't call him a liar because I was the one who invented the blasted bells.

He, impishly, rang another non-bell for the porter who came to carry my non-bags, which were heavy. I gave him a lavish non-tip and we all sat down to dissect the performances. The intelligent lecturer kept uttering the word 'orgueil'. Was I too proud? Was the receptionist too haughty?

When I was leaving, I thanked them warmly for their welcome, wished them well and told them my next stop was at the Ustinov house on this side of Lake Geneva.

'Are you still playing the game?' asked a girl.

'Well. In a way I am. And then again, I am not,' and, in a way, that was not true and, in another way, it was.

★　　★　　★

You can hear three sounds from Peter Ustinov's terrace. There's a train at the bottom of the valley. In Switzerland trains swish through places that are flat, and climb up places that aren't. They don't thunder. They make a soft, furry sound, as though they were sliding on fine oil. The second sound was mechanical too. But a new sound, the sound of a tractor especially equipped to trim a vineyard. This is a sputtering sound, a fussy sound, as though a machine has developed a particular worry about an individual branch of the vine, and is worrying with it. In the days of the earlier traveller, there would have been no train, and the vines would have been tended by a woman with a stooping back and a big basket. The third sound would, however, be easily recognised. The ubiquitous cow bell. There in the field, a herd of tawny cows and their huge, almost prison-like bells.f

With a man of Ustinov's stature, and I speak here of artistic achievement and not of girth, you would expect a much grander demesne. This is the sort of house which might be occupied by a reasonably successful bank manager, in a Zürich branch. There are plenty of rooms, each one facing the wide panorama of the Lake and the Alps beyond, but the rooms are cluttered with the necessary props of a man who is also a scholar, and a musician, and an historian, and a comedian, and a bon viveur. There seem to be piles of new books and old records everywhere. There are plenty of machines to make music. A big shiny black piano, and banks of stereophony. The garden is dominated by an immense satellite dish, tilted to the sun, or the stars, depending on the time of day. It is an odd sight, since everything is rural, if not almost suburban.

'It's the only dish round here that won't go in the kitchen.'

Ustinov, even though it was warm and sunny, had apparently spent the entire morning in his study, clamped to

Satellite dish, tree and Ustinov. Lake Geneva

the television set, receiving pictures of the American Senate investigations into Irangate. The pictures were live, direct, beamed out of Washington and collected, like electronic dew, in his garden dish.

'Problem is,' he says with a grin, 'all these generals and senators and everybody now know how entertaining they all are. And they've started over-acting. The generals are more generals than ever I remember generals being in the army. I speak here as a private, so I had rather an El Greco view of generals.

'We live, don't we, in times where we have the most extraordinary means of communication, but we haven't yet thought of anything better to say to each other.'

This throws me a little. I was about to ask exactly where we were sitting, and I didn't mean in his garden. I meant to ask for identification of places on the opposite shore, and where, for instance, was Evian, and its health club.

'Where are we, then?'

I should have known better.

'We're in my garden Russell (with exaggerated Northern accent), and over there (pronounced 'thur') you can just catch a glimpse of the outskirts of Rochdale in all that industrial smog.'

Ustinov takes the sting out of his own tale by laughing at himself as well as at you, the victim. I have known this wizard for quite a time now. Early in this manifestation of my career, he took me to Westminster School, to talk about his first days, and to hang colourful robes upon the long-gone, desiccated masters. What he doesn't know, he makes up, and only he knows the difference and, sometimes, even that is doubtful. He is the arch-Wheldon Mariner. His mind flits across the surface of a conversation but, unlike so many of the rest of us, his mouth has already refined the instant thought.

'The bloody car burnt to a cinder last Wednesday on the freeway. I wasn't in it, mind you. It's been in the garage for nine days and nobody from the insurance has been anywhere near it. That's why I am agitated,' he said, sitting like a full Buddha and showing absolutely no sign of agitation. 'They're sitting on the dough, taking the interest on it. The only thing I found in the car was a programme of a play called *Joan of Arc at the Stake*! Maybe that's what set it off.' A non-agitated chuckle.

My old enemy, the sun, was now at its fiercest height. Horrid. And the only shade cast was behind the satellite dish, and I would have looked even more foolish shouting from behind the ironmongery. This same glutton sun, which had burned me into a crisped sulk in the early days, now frying me again. I asked Peter if we could go inside. He looked agitated, for the first time.

'Because I'm burning,' I said.

'All right, Harty, I'll take you to a climate you're more used to. I'll turn off the heating.' I ran in, and he pottered behind, making tutting noises of incomprehension.

Naturally we talked about travel, and I tried to explain that, on the whole, I prefer to be driven than to drive, and he disagreed, wholeheartedly.

'I don't care for just sitting in a car, looking out of a window. What's the point? I have a 1934 Hispano Suisa, 12 cylinder, nine and a half litre, and the only thing that works perfectly is the speaking tube leading from the old lady at the back, who happens to be *my* old lady, and connects with the chauffeur, who happens to be me. And she bellows down this, "Stop here." It makes a tremendous noise. It was a car that needed a driver with a sense of humour, because when

Bond Street was still a two-way traffic system, I couldn't turn into it with one turn, and I had to reverse and then inch back, and keep doing it, and all the buses behind me had to do the same thing. It was hilarious. And it's fun to be at the wheel of a car where you can look down at a bus driver and wish him "Good morning".'

There is home-grown wine here, chez Ustinov. Some cool bottles are brought to the table. I should point out here that this is a properly lived-in house. Nobody flies into a domestic panic if a wet ring from the bottle bottom forms upon a surface. Nor does any fusspot run out with a miserable little coaster upon which to balance a chalice. I speak with feeling since I get agitated at rings on surfaces, and I am the one who hops about with coasters. It is a pleasure, sometimes, not to look into a mirror.

As I have wandered through Switzerland, and prepare to have the leaving treatments before I go underground to Italy, I deem it to be a sensible time to check on the still unset conclusions I have reached. Ustinov helps to make the smallest suggestions to my mould.

'The Swiss are rather like the Scots, without access to the sea. All this idea of hotels and banks, institutions of that sort, came to them by bitter experience. Don't forget that, in the Middle Ages, they were the highest paid mercenaries in Europe. Otherwise the Pope would hardly have had Swiss guards. They were extremely tough and rugged fighters. Suddenly they came to the conclusion that they were fighting each other. They were hired as an élite corps and their brothers were hired by the enemy, and there they were fighting each other, for money. So they got together and said, this is ridiculous. There must be another way. So they thought of peaceful things, like banks and hotels. At the same time, they have a sense of humour about themselves. They aren't the dour souls we like to pretend they are . . .

'There's a story of God creating Switzerland and being enchanted with the sight of his first-made milkmaid. "I say," he said, "I am God the Father. Could I have a glass of your delicious milk?" And she said, "Oh, Monsieur, you deserve a glass of milk what with creating all this and everything." And she gave him the glass and said, "That will be three francs, fifty, thank you.'''

Ustinov, with an eye and an ear on the timing of any public performance, introduces the subject of humour. You don't readily associate the natives of this neutral land with madness and laughter. You would be surprised, he says.

'Switzerland, true, doesn't have one tremendous sense of fun. At least, not a ready sense. And yet, nevertheless, has produced some of the world's greatest clowns. Grock was Swiss, and there's a genius here now called Dmitri. And a whole school of them. That is something overlooked when everyone staggers about talking of the gnomes of Zürich. What about the gnomes of Bertram Mills?

'And you have to have a sense of humour when you're surrounded by impregnable mountains. Which is why the Swiss are such good tunnellers, you know. They've made an art of getting out of the place. Consider the alternative. If you live in the Netherlands or the Steppes, you have to create your own scenery. And people it with your imagination. That's why the great fairy tales of Europe come from Flanders and Russia. Flat. Flat. And unfunny.'

As the afternoon wears on, there are calls from publishers and agents, and there is the insistent American broadcasting service in the next room. The door to the satellite receiver is half open, and Ustinov has half an eye cocked on it. You can tell that he doesn't want to miss anything in the turmoil of this vast and busy world which surrounds him. He can't afford to do that. He is a miller. And everything that floats in the aether and runs along the ground is his grist. Travellers tend to swap tales. I love stories about mad hotels and daft showers and rude concierges, and the drama that frequently unfolds behind a thin dividing bedroom wall.

'The filthiest toilet I ever did see,' he says, 'was in Algiers. Filthy. But just visible out of what we should call the grime was a notice which read "Please leave this place as you find it." I needed no such bidding,' and the substantial frame quivers with mirth.

I have not been at all sure about language in Switzerland. In Germany it was a hard and sometimes distressing experience trying to understand how one long and unpronounceable word could really contain so much meaning.

Here, I have run in and out of recognisable zones of language. A restaurant, for instance, will have a menu printed in two or three languages.

'There are four,' says the resident philologist. 'There's French, which they speak like the French. Then there's Italian which sounds like . . . er . . . well, Italian. The German has a kind of medieval patina over it. Then there's this hybrid, albeit an ancient one, called Romansh. It's an interesting language. Used by a minority, but there are enough of them now to have their own radio programme between three and four in the afternoon. It was left behind by the Roman legions, you know. When Rome fell, the poor soldiers were left stranded up these valleys. It's rather a haunting idea, really. It's almost Latin. With a dash of Roumanian. If you go to look for the "Mens' Room", it says "Homens", which really outdoes the Latin at its own game. It sounds as if it has been invented. Like ancient Esperanto.

'And yet, and yet, for all this mix, for all this international Red Cross thing, and private accounts, it's really rather a pleasingly parochial place. Let me show you now. There was this Swiss gentleman looking at the fountain in Geneva, that huge singular spout. Suddenly, he notices that he is not alone. Standing next to him is an extremely African gentleman. He's looking up at the fountain too. This colour of native is sufficiently remarkable for the Swiss man to make a double, a triple, a quadruple, a quintuple take. He tries to work it all out and, eventually, says to him, "You're not from here, are you?" And the black gentleman says, "No, you're right. I'm from Lausanne." That's a glimpse of Swiss village life.

'Good God, that's Ollie North! Come on, let's go and watch what the rest of the world is doing!'

So much for the concept of the village life of Peter Ustinov in Switzerland plugged into the universe.

★   ★   ★

I am beginning to wake from this dream. Have I travelled up and down mountains, through valleys and meadows? Why, every time I close my eyes, do cow bells ring? Have I, perhaps, died? I cannot open my mouth to breathe. I can see the white walls of what appears to be a cell, but there is no blue Chagall hanging there.

The mummification process is almost finished. Of course, I am being rejuvenated in the Royal Health Club in Evian. If memory serves me, that is where the retrospective wandering began. The wardress is coming to crack the plaster. It is impossible to laugh, barely possible to smile, just possible to recall, lying here in such an absurd posture, Dorothy Parker's remark: 'They threw away the mould before they made him!' The thirst is appalling. Oh, for a beakerful of the warm South . . . as in Italy!

CHAPTER
SEVEN

Whoever designed and drew the border between Switzerland and Italy knew exactly what he was doing. You travel into the appalling noise and diesel smell of the Mont Blanc tunnel and then, suddenly, spot a pin-prick of what could be sunlight. The fresh air smacks your reconstituted face and the road, onwards, looks as though it is going to tumble down into the valley of Courmayeur. The psychology of pleasure is exactly reflected in the dramatic geography. We have spent an instructive, intriguing time 'up' in Switzerland. Now the Grand Tourist catches his first distant prospect of the ultimate goal, 'down' there in Italy.

Even, heaven help us, the motor car knows what is happening. The engine is infected. The same motor that worked hard in the High Alps suggests, with a satirical hum, that you can take your foot off the accelerator and let it go!

As ever, the language and the money present the first obstacle. Though these days, some three-quarters of the intended journey having been taken, words and bits of paper are not so daunting as they were. In Italy, the money is as operatic a concept as a meal or a firework display. It's a hard job to divide or multiply anything by two and a half thousand, especially when the taxi-driver is fuming or the automatic toll-gate is flashing across the motorway. At moments like these, you come to understand the contemporary pressures on the traveller. Your eighteenth-century horse wouldn't start ticking with a string of zeros. At moments like these, too, you come to realise that you are not the great European jetsetter you may have imagined. Panic is a powerful propeller. And panic, although seemingly controlled, is ever present, just below the surface, but not at all subterranean. I think I have over-tipped like an idiot in most places so far. But in Italy I am sure that I have made a significant contribution to the welfare of thousands. I have, by panic again, inadvertently paid off mortgages, bought people new tyres, scattered a shopful of deep freezes and, perhaps, set up Anna and Giovanni in a small vineyard in Lucca. So keen have I been to please. So nervous of their response. So slow at mental arithmetic.

The problem of language has a different emphasis. I can recognise words. I can make myself understood in the same basics. But I haven't learned to argue, to fight or to defend. So no matter what moral principle is debated, I am automatically on the wrong channel.

My dear friend in Yorkshire called Madge Hindle is an actress. In *Spotlight*, the theatre's *Who's Who*, she appears as 'flame-haired, tempestuous, ex-Mayoress of Blackburn'. You should see her operate in Italy. She can't speak a word. She can't understand one either, and yet she gets all she wants and sometimes more than she needs. She utters long lines of pretend 'cornetto' Italian. And everything ends in 'azione' or 'izione' and it is meaningless. Crowds part. Waiters rush. Barriers open. It is quite a performance. But it doesn't work when I try.

Therefore, on the evening of the day upon which I have gently descended from the northern Italian Alps, I have arrived in Bergamo. The centre of this ancient place is a well-preserved, handsome small city. But on high. Citt 'Alta'. It is a characteristic of most northern Italian cities. However fiery and mad this reasonably new nation seems to be, someone, somewhere, has put the stamp of preservation on an official document. You can build away to your heart's content at the outer edges of a civilised complex. But you must not touch history. The old town is a place for people to live in, and walk and talk in. The new town, anywhere, is often the place to work in. So it doesn't matter if it's brutal and ugly, so long as it's functional.

Bergamo comes with starry recommendations. Alan Bennett lies down and thinks there rather a lot. But he had not prepared me for the size of the old city. It seems as though crusaders have just left to conquer some other poor infidels. Towers and crenellations, and public buildings of a solid and prosperous dimension.

In the middle of the square there is, on this warm evening, a Punch and Judy show. It is, like almost everything else, a family affair. Like the cinema, and the restaurant and any old juke-box café, and Mass, and weddings and funerals. No one is too young to be a part, and no one considered too old. Punch and Judy don't need language. They just need sticks and savagery. The children do not seem to be abused or disturbed by this public act of gratuitous violence. And if your Granny is laughing and sitting next to you, then it is all right for you to laugh too.

At this time of the year, everyone drinks iced tea. Ruth Donadoni drinks a lot of it. She lives in Bergamo, with her Italian husband. Cardiff was OK. That's where she was born. But this beats the south wetlands of Wales, where it's always too cold to serve iced tea, and where, in any case, tea is too sanctified a British beverage to allow any questionable continental habits to creep into its preparation. Ruth Donadoni is a teacher of English in her own language school. Her methods in my instruction are very useful and unorthodox.

'The first and almost only lesson is to look people in the eye, then they will take you seriously. Don't be shy. Don't look down when you've grabbed a waiter's attention or the lady in the shop. Speak right at them. You know how lots of English people find it embarrassing to talk at people, and they constantly look over your shoulder, and all that nonsense. Well. It doesn't wash here.'

This is sound advice. But what do you do once you have locked your eyes to theirs? Ideally, there should be a fluid stream of orders and requests, but you can't keep staring at someone whilst you rack your brain for the right word, and then get even more agitated by trying to construct a sentence which is grammatically sound enough to contain this, as yet, hidden word.

'Oh, you don't need words,' says the bubbling Ruth. 'Words aren't *that* important. You use gestures. Use your hands, your arms, your eyebrows. It's what they call in England "gesticulating". You can express almost anything. Desire (a slightly rude gesture, with one crooked left arm and the right hand clamped quickly on the muscle of the left). Disgust. (This with the mouth.) Indifference. The declarations of annoyance and disapproval. Delight. Despair.' (Why, I wonder, do so many of the basic emotions begin with 'D'?)

It will, I think and hope, become obvious that once you have left that essentially private land called Switzerland, and responded to the echo call of Italy, you have, in fact, entered a theatre. Everything that Ruth has told me so far indicates a degree of performance.

'Look at them all, walking about in the evening air. They're all performers. They are all part of a mildly exaggerated drama. And the further south you go, the more dramatic the gesture. Don't be put off. Join in. They'll like that. They think we are starchy and reserved.'

Which is, of course, what one, regrettably, is. The advice, ultimately to prove most useful, rolls out of the Welsh oracle.

'Traffic lights . . . well. Some red lights are redder than others. Don't stop at them all. You'll never get there. Think on your feet, or behind your wheel. I mean, if you stop at every red light, an awful lot of people will bang into the back of you, and scream at you for being so stupid. What's the point of stopping at a red light if there's nothing coming across you. Never, ever, stop at what looks like a zebra crossing to let someone cross the road. You see, what happens then is the driver behind you comes flashing out, impatiently, and knocks over the person you've stopped for, and then sues you for obstruction. It's mad, isn't it!'

It is. It is mad. It is also, in some odd way, liberating. Her final words were equally encouraging.

'When you arrive in Italy, you should try to do everything

you've always wanted to do in England and never dared. But without being official about it. If you don't ask anybody but get on and do it, they'll close the official eye. If you start being all English, you know, "Would you mind awfully if I . . .?", then they'll throw the book at you, and put on a uniform.

'And, finally, it's best to have an audience. Wait till you see three or four people hanging around and then have a scene . . . in a shop, say, or at the booking office . . . or the bank. Don't start shouting till there's a crowd. They'll love it, and, eventually, so will you. Arriverderci.'

That, in a sense, was the overture. The programme notes, as it were.

The first act is a near nightmare, in Barga. In times of stress, that is to say, just before a performance of 'Harty in Italy', I head straight for somewhere or someone I know. Ten years ago, I'd never heard of Barga. Then my blessed old friend, William Walton, ex-Oldham, Freeman of that borough, composer, Member of the Order of Merit, told me that his one-act opera, *The Bear*, was to be performed by music students at a home-made festival in this little Italian town, and did I want to go? I did. We got merrily drunk every night and the opera seemed magical, and I didn't remember much else about the place except that it had a fine primitive air. We were there just before the creeping hand of restoration had laid hold. Just before little antique shops, next door to the local arts and crafts men, sprang out of a parched earth, and were over-watered by new wealth and commercial prosperity. In other words, Barga was a little 'run-down'. You should see it now. Everything seems a newly washed gold, and if you penetrate the mysteries of the back passages (sic), you can be coolly sprayed with the drifts of water that come from machines which blast the grime of history from dwellings that were built long before anyone thought of a Grand Tour.

Thank God that they, whoever they are, haven't yet started washing the people. There is a splendid bar, tobacconist, sandwich shop, stamp outlet, small universal emporium in the middle of the irregular square. Aristodemo is the proprietor. They probably built the whole thing around him.

He said he remembered me. But with a television camera fixed steadily upon his Latin face, it is hardly likely that he would have played dumb. When the lights went on, he started his wholly acceptable exaggerated performance.

'Cheeeps sheeeeez.'

'What?'

'Ah! (hands thrown up) Mama mia. Ay sey cheeeeps sheeeez!'

If this is a play, I have lost the script, or forgotten it.

'Cheeeeps sheeeez? What eez it?' I ask in a stupidly neo-Italian accent.

'Eeez sheeeez from cheeeeps.'

This unenlightening encounter could have continued all day. A customer, another Italian with a Scottish burr, holding a stiff fish under his arm, taking it home to the wife to be thawed for lunch, helped us out of this linguistic cul-de-sac.

'He says you want piece of sheeeep's cheeeese?!'

'Si, si, si,' bubbles Aristodemo. 'Cheeeeps sheeeez.' I summon up all Ruth Donadoni's advice, stare straight into his frustrated eyes, and try to teach him how to pronounce these words in English. Why on earth he should want to learn, or me to teach, I haven't yet analysed.

This basic Italian grocer's shop is like all the busy shops of my childhood. Candles, matches, starch, butter, sugar, lard, pasta . . . no, not pasta. I don't think anyone had heard of pasta in post-war Blackburn. And if they had, it would have been branded as foreign muck. And, what is worse, Italian. Of course we'd heard of spaghetti and macaroni. They came in proper Heinz tins and you'd never call them bits of 'pasta'. Pasta was the basic food of another enemy, the Italians. How is it, I wonder, that the Italians were never really 'the enemy'? In the school yard, there was always a towering and offensive bully. Behind his back you would call him 'Hitler'. He was the real enemy. Then there was always another lad who would hold Hitler's coat whilst he bashed you. You called him 'Mussolini'. Sometimes, you could hear him say, 'You hit him, Brian (or Eric), I'll hold your coat.' And when you lifted your bloody head, and collected the loose teeth from behind the dustbins in the playground, you cursed

Hitler but never Mussolini.

I have tried to persuade myself that the Italians were acting the part of our enemy. No one who lives off cheeeeps sheeeez can lay serious claim to international belligerence.

I am beginning to be infected with something I may have to describe as 'bravura'. Good God, I have even undone the second shirt button, and this morning I seriously entertained the possibility of not wearing socks. The most alarming manifestation of this disease, if, indeed, it is so serious, is a fresh approach to driving. My foot seems to be fastened to the accelerator, as if by a determined macho glue. This works reasonably well when the streets are straight and the traffic is relatively light. It lands me in terrible trouble as I say farewell to Aristodemo. Barga is a tight town. Right angles push hard against other right angles. There is no curve or sweep here. You can't jam down your foot, as in Florence or Rome, and lean to your left, as you slide round a circus.

I left Aristo's shop at half-past twelve of a hot morning. I arrived at the gate of Barga, less than half a mile away, one hour later. Hot is too cold a word to describe my body temperature. Hot is too cool a word to describe my temper. I was inflamed. The car jammed at the first corner, and no amount of to-ing and fro-ing would release me from the intransigent iron-grip of the buildings. I remember a mad moment when I thought to myself . . . 'Ah, well, this ancient town wishes to hold me here, loathe to let me go . . .' That was the combinedly lunatic conclusion of sunstroke, wine and sheep's cheese.

People came from near but not, I hope, from far, to witness this purple-faced traveller, trapped in a smart car in an old street. Children and old men, young men and maidens, the mayor, women going to the laundrette, the bank manager on his way to a businessman's pasta, half of the population came to witness this increasingly manic scene. And the bigger the audience, the bolder my pointless rocking of the immobilised machine.

At one hot point, I had thought to climb out, since the door could not be opened, and leave the wretched lump of tin wedged across the street. Maybe, in the process of time, someone would build a bridge over it, and people might come to visit this strange deposit of a former not-so-Grand Tourist. All Ruth's instructions about engaging peoples' eyes, and gesticulating, and waiting until there was some kind of audience seemed to be of little use. I'd done all those things. The audience was growing bigger but nothing was happening.

An old man, two cheeky schoolboys and the yaps of a discouraging hound finally prised me out of Barga, and embarrassment. The temperature in the low nineties and my own temper tipped beyond boiling point. It is marginally amusing to look back upon this lost hour's push-me/pull-you. It was not amusing at the time. Aristodemo, hitherto my friend, had gone back into his shop and, for the first time since the end of the war, closed for lunch.

★   ★   ★

Cars run, or get stuck, on petrol. The rest of the nation gets by smoothly with the liberal lubrication of olive oil. 'What did you see on your Tour, then?' people started to ask me shortly after I had finished, and I get a perverse pleasure from saying 'Oh, I went to a false teeth factory in Liechtenstein, and I spent a morning in an olive oil factory near Lucca with an Italian Count whose family is part of the Worthington beer clan.' And they pause for a moment and sigh and say, 'I see.' Then I tell them other things.

Count Tadini lives in a grand family villa near the walled city of Lucca. He lives alone, except for the languid peacocks by the lake and memories of richer times. He speaks perfect English. There was no need to gesticulate.

'My old English governess, Miss Ramage, Anglo-Irish, actually would be pleased to hear your compliment. She gave us English dictation and made us learn Christopher Robin, and persuaded us to read *Winnie the Pooh*.'

Here is a really civilised European. The iced tea is served in the overgrown but handsome garden. Inside, a little treasure house of old family albums and original passports, handwritten, signed by Lord Clarendon, and Palmerston. The word 'Tobler' also appears in the scrolled documents. The word 'Toblerone' springs to mind. I mean, with 'Worthington' on the one hand and 'Toblerone' on the other, we are suddenly peering into a secret garden of very big business. This inquiry is brushed lightly to one side.

Odd other things bob to the surface.

'That is a picture of my godson.' The picture reveals a man clearly older than his godfather.

'He's, now, well . . . 93.'

I've never seen a film called *The Garden of the Finzi-Continis*, but this title keeps charging a part of my brain. There must have been peacocks and iced tea and passports, and now this, a 93-year-old godson. There is an explanation. He is an English neighbour who, in the early evening of his life (and what time precisely is that, I wonder?) converted to Catholicism, and asked Count Tadini to sponsor him. The reason is not as romantic as a million other strange family possibilities.

Olive oil isn't romantic either. It is one of the oldest and most natural of Italian medicines; now it is a fashionable salad dressing. We went to see the great Bertolli factory which lies outside Lucca. Huge truck loads of olives grind in at one end and tins of the refined liquid are loaded at the other. It is a question of filtering and re-filtering, and filtering again.

'Take the glass.' The Count hands me a large glass of brown oil – a little like the machine oil that drips off large turbines.

'Take a mouthful of air first. You must have a big mouth and full of air . . . right? . . . and take a big mouthful of oil . . . right? . . . and roll it round . . . right? Can you taste spice and fresh flavour and . . . a little sunshine and earth?' I spat the oil, with the sun and the spice and the earth, into the nearest bucket. The Count swallowed his. The memory of castor oil lies too deep for me to be wandering around Europe swallowing large glasses of oil and pretending to enjoy it.

There is virgin oil, a purer substance after its pressings. Then there is extra-virgin oil.

'How can a virgin be an extra-virgin?' I ask, not altogether naively. 'How can you be just a little bit pregnant? Either it's virgin, or it isn't.'

'It is a classification,' the stern Count replies. 'And a question of acidity,' he adds. 'And the colour is a green-yellow, and clear. There is not a hint of left-over paste.' He gargles and gargles again. Rather magisterially. He is about to swallow another mouthful.

I said, 'I think it smells like bacon.'

I left shortly after I realised that the Count, instead of swallowing, spat.

★ ★ ★

Two reasons for including a visit to Milan at this stage. I wanted to see *The Last Supper*, and by certain little devious social tricks, had arranged a meeting with Giorgio Armani, one of the contemporary heroes of Europe. Whether vast crowds will stand in patient queues to look at a piece of material designed and fashioned by Armani in another five hundred years is a matter for the idlest speculation. The power of Leonardo's attraction is indisputable. And growing. Education and film and Kenneth Clark (and a lot of money from Japan) have made sure of a limitless extent to his reputation.

Milan in the early morning. A lousy breakfast of bitter black coffee and bread rolls tasting of stale and hardened cotton wool. The Italians cannot cope with breakfast. Unless, of course, it is not important to them. I like the rituals of breakfast almost anywhere in the world. I like to potter in my room and be lazy, and read a little and write a card or a note. I will not, as a matter of pig-headed principle, fill in a breakfast order, on a long card with a hole at the top, designed to fit on to the outer knob of the bedroom door. I don't like putting ticks into little boxes. The Americans started all that, and it is too constricting, too organised, too intransigent, especially at an early hour. When you go to bed at, say, midnight, having had an expansive evening, with good food and good company, how can you know that, at exactly quarter to eight, you will want muesli and kippers? How do you then know that the night will not have been spent tossing and turning? And that all you need is coffee and fresh melon? I prefer to telephone the order, even if it is misunderstood. Whether the coffee is good or mud, there is always the consequent nail-breaking fiddle with little packs of butter and unopenable tin foil pots of jam. If there is a but-

153

ter mountain, why don't European hoteliers help to dispose of it by serving small foothills of the stuff on visitors' breakfast plates?

My Milanese hotel is a well-run factory for passing travellers. The bedroom is like a private room in a clinic. Everything works. There is no picture on the walls. There are no curtains. There are electric blinds. A proper and experienced working mind has gone into its planning. But no soul.

No matter. Leonardo da Vinci had soul enough from which the rest of the world could gather comfort and confirmation. The comfort of the uplifting of the human spirit – even to the designing of an early aircraft. The confirmation of man's new-found position at the centre of the universe – which, this bright morning, is Milan.

Leaving, therefore, the dull sublunary thoughts of coffee and bread behind, I set out to see *The Last Supper*.

Here I would like to be able to describe a profound spiritual experience. There haven't been too many so far. Moments of amazement, of wonder and annoyance. But nothing, apart from the disturbing encounter with Sister Scholastica in Germany, nothing to persuade me to go home and lie down in a dark room, and ponder the futility of existence.

All this I say by way of lessening my own remembered shock. When I got to the Church of Santa Maria delle Grazie, now the tabernacle of Leonardo's masterpiece, it was closed for the day. There is, therefore, nothing more to say. I met an American wedding party, doing their own version of the Grand Tour. We fell, together, into disappointed conversation until the bridegroom saw a café across the road. We trooped off to assuage our temporary sorrows. I had a large beer, sitting, as I was, under a reproduction, in pasty shades, of Leonardo's *Last Supper*. They sell the same print in the Medici Galleries, in Bond Street.

The Armani experience was much more illuminating. He was in one sense 'open', and in another wholly 'closed'. Applications for an audience have to be placed in good time. Signor Armani knows perfectly well where he is at any given day on the calendar, but you cannot switch this kind of tour to Sydney, Tokyo, New York. This is the big time. I count it as a measure of ultimate success if you can arrange your life so that you don't have to travel to work. Armani has gathered everything together, under the roof of a huge, discreet palazzo in Milan. He lives there or, more precisely, he has a large apartment there. There are palatial bolt-holes elsewhere. In the country. On the odd island. That kind of thing. Here, in Milan, the office, the drawing-room (i.e. the room where he makes his drawings), is one floor below. The salon is below that. Everything has a strong flavour of Japanese super-efficiency. The floors are polished. The elevator always seems to be standing to attention at the floor you require.

Every powerful man has a much more powerful woman standing in front of him. Think of the Duke of Edinburgh. Think of Ex-Presidents Marcos and Roosevelt. Think of the Duke of Windsor, and Duff Cooper. Think of George Formby. Beryl Formby would never let him out of her sight. He might have burned his ukulele or looked at another woman! Giorgio Armani has an extraordinarily handsome and persuasively Scandinavian lady who monitors each move, *after* she has decided whether it is diplomatic, advantageous, or just possibly enjoyable. This kind of prodigiously powerful PR officer does not grow on any known tree. Her name doesn't appear on any available list. You can't hire her services from an agency. She is not Armani's wife or lover. She's too important to be a part of the whimsical caravanserai that finds its purpose in the heady drag of fame.

"Armani will see you at 11.00.' This is an order from a high command. What it means is, 'You will see Armani at 11.00.' No equivocation. No ifs and buts.

The private apartments are not to my taste. That means nothing. It means, simply, that if I could transpose my head (but not my body) and place it on Giorgio's frame, I would not surround myself by such expensive austerity. This is 'nouvelles ameubles' (or nouveau ameublement). A large minimalist apartment. Huge sliding windows lead to a terrace, which any proud northern housewife would grace with the adjective 'patio'. Very low sofas. Fine once you are prostrate but hell to go up and down into. The one flight of carefully controlled fantasy is a large old rocking horse, standing in the window. The only disarray to carpets and cushions is provided by a small predatory army of cats. It all chimes. You know, before he arrives, that the carefully designed shape of this successful life can only be altered by a non-human influence. The rest of us are almost aching for someone to make a dent in the plumped cushions. Not Armani. No thank you. There is a grand plan. Cats, though they make demands, do not make assumptions.

Armani is five minutes late. That puts me into a frightfully bouncy mood. The Ice-Queen precedes him. That makes me doubtful. He is smaller than I am. That restores my confidence. He is under-dressed in what even I, in my colour blindness, can see are shades of blue. That binds me to him. Every time I buy a new suit, it is blue. Dark blue. That is the only advantage I gained from going to Oxford. And that is not the whole truth.

I was going to say we then sat down. He sat down. She sank down, and I subsided, rather like an old block of flats in the process of demolition. She defined the parameters of the conversation, unwittingly, by saying that Signor Armani could not speak English and, therefore, the dialogue would pass through her. So, as we started, I spoke English to her, she spoke Italian to him, he replied to her in French. She translated this into English. I think this was a game. Gradually, something of a friendly nature grew out of this bizarre impromptu of a United Nations Assembly. Armani could not resist the odd English word. Easier to convey the precision of an idea.

If you bestride the world of fashion, like a Colossus, it appears that your first obligation is to diversify, as a form of life insurance. Ars, in this job, is not necessarily longa, and vita still remains brevis. I have noticed this with Conran, Bruce Oldfield, St Laurent, Zandra Rhodes. Once you have grabbed the hungry attention of those whose will is to form fashion's vanguard, then you must give them tights, jewellery and perfume. You must encapsulate them in Armani so that, for one profitable moment of time, you have full copyright on a body. This is not a moral judgment. Heaven help us. That we should be so fortunately influential. It is an amateur sociological observation.

Looking at an artist work is more satisfying than talking about it. I was intrigued by the whole philosophy of minimalism. Buttons cut off. Collars stripped away. Like someone in high summer deliberately picking the leaves off a fully flowered tree and, in a perverse way, seeking to expose the skeleton. Armani's original models, wearing his original clothes, were barely anatomised.

'If you drive this theory to its ultimate, what do you finish with?'

Armani looks at the Princess PR. She can't translate something he already understands. The Englishness of his exclusive petticoats begins to appear.

'I have stripped enough. Now I am thinking of putting it all back again.' ('Reculer,' as Boileau would have said in a different philosophical vein, 'pour mieux sauter.')

I began to wonder about Armani's own body. It seems a serious issue. After all, if you devote your entire artistic and commercial energies to the decoration of the frames of other people, where, in a sense, does that leave you?

He's a small man. Maybe five foot six. I have already seen a great deal of sophisticated equipment in a private gymnasium. I am mesmerised by the amount of money and time people will expend upon that which I have now resigned myself to describing as 'a sagging parcel of flesh'. Armani's body is a whiplash of contained energy. You can rake your critical eye up and down the corporeal frame. There isn't, I am sad to relate, an ounce of visible spare flesh. I should take this as an example, an exhortation, if not a warning. But all that I can think of is King Canute. The tide, governed by a power greater than man, eventually comes in, and a harvest has to be gathered. Some vicious god, at a day of human tax-gathering, will not consider the glory of your pectorals or the neatness of your waist. You will not need to be too percipient to realise that these thoughts are not prompted by mortality; simply envy. ('What was the most important lesson you learned on your Grand Tour, Russell' They will ask. And I shall have to say, 'If you really want the truth, and who really does, it was the bleak recognition of envy!')

The domestic details of young Giorgio's life read like those of everyone else I know. It's all to do with houseproud mothers. Mothers who dusted coal before placing the nuggets on to the pyramidical fire. Mothers who would have slapped you if, in later life, you were to have accused them of possessing a 'lace curtain' mentality. Giorgio's mother and mine would have spoken the same language. We don't. Except through a third person. And then we don't.

With half a serious smile I then conclude: 'If you were to be given any God-like quality (and God knows, he has that already) and could re-design yourself, what would you look like'

There is a long pause. A cat scratches at the tasselled edges of a Kilim. Yawns. Lies down.

'I would be . . . tall . . . and the same.'

'Taller?'

'No. Just tall.'

And then we are lost again in the marshlands of philology where even our watchful interpreteuse cannot be of any assistance.

There are a million attractive features about Armani. I like the fact that he says he never goes out. He may well go out every night and quaff and carouse until the third cock's crow, but I like the idea that he says he doesn't.

I like his space-age bathroom. Personally, I would be afraid of leaving a rim round the liner of a bath, and I couldn't take a shower in a bathroom which has one wall serving as a two-way mirror. I am suspicious of Scandinavian lighting. I don't like polished floors, or doors that turn on a central pivot and not on a hinge. But, here I am, behaving in the most selfishly proprietorial manner. And I am only one hour's supplicant. And why should I think, in a moment of entire abandon, that my dog could eat his cats.

One thing is certain. I have spent some time, dangerous and enjoyable, with a radiator. I have an inflexible rule (to be bent, as all good rules may be) which states that people can be readily divided into two categories. 'Drains' and 'radiators'. Armani is no drain.

On my last day in Milan, I went to Upim which is a cross between Woolworth and British Home Stores. I bought a summer jacket for £18. I tell everybody that it is an Armani jacket and, thank God, they are well-mannered enough not to demand an inspection of the label. The paradox is that, when I wear it, it doesn't look as though it has been designed by Armani for me. But, since I have deceivingly invoked such a powerful name, nobody has yet dared to question this claim. That is power!

★   ★   ★

Armani has put me in good humour. Not high humour. But he has livened me, alerted me. Here is another instance, and these instances are growing in number if not in significance, that questions are not necessarily to be answered. But it is important to ask them.

Derek Bailey has been an important influence in my life. He is directing the cameras which are following this tour. There are times when he suggests the next destination. Suggests but does not dictate. I know him well enough, and he me, to know that, if he suggests a détour to the Benedictine Abbey at Einsiedeln, it would be stupid to ignore his advice. He is, after all, directing this Tour in more than one obvious sense. The original young Tourists equipped themselves with a 'bear leader' – a man of some wisdom and experience who was used to the staging posts.

In the olden days, of course, you would need a 'bear leader'. There were no reliable maps. There were no telephones or telexes. How could you plan an overnight stay in Lyon if you did not know where to change your exhausted horses? We are talking now of a time before Mr Cook made a business out of touring. The world and, in particular, Europe, has become a familiar place. At six o'clock, on any normal evening, you can watch events unfold in Rome and Tokyo. We are neighbours in the sense that we are given a licensed glimpse into each other's back yards. There is little mystery left in crossing the Alps, and that turns me, in the self-imposed role of traveller, more towards the changing people who live on the roadside of the Grand Tour than any pressing concern with the route itself. People have a consistent and annoying habit of dying. You have to trap them when you can. Their monuments remain. The Victoria & Albert now houses a collection of Schiaparelli frocks but I don't know whether Schiaparelli was a he or a she, and whether they had polished floors. The emphasis of my personal Tour places the people firmly in the foreground. The background will remain the background, after I have passed through it, and beyond.

When Derek Bailey says to you, in a noisy street outside the Palazzo Armani in Milan, that he knows Verdi's great-great granddaughter – Lodovica Verdi – is at home in the family house in Busetto, and he's quite prepared to drive me over, and I'll be charmed, then there is only one serious question.

Will she be charmed, or even remotely interested, by my call?

I need not have worried. Lodovica Verdi. Grand, round name. She is, maybe, eighteen or nineteen years old, apple-cheeked, wide-eyed, handsome and most warmly welcoming. Verdi's house sits in the middle of rich fields and is surrounded by smells. Smells of lavender and rosemary and lilies. It is not a grand house. I am not even sure that it qualifies as a villa – whatever proportions that may need for its title.

I am disadvantaged by this encounter. I know the Verdi *Requiem* by heart, sideways and backwards, for all the wrong reasons which then become the right ones. In my earlier days, I was asked to organise a performance of the *Requiem* in St Paul's Cathedral, with the London Symphony Orchestra and four international soloists and Leonard Bernstein on the shaky podium. The enterprise was directed by Humphrey Burton, for television. At the end of this stupefying performance, he came running to the back of the Cathedral, saying that there would have to be several short pieces re-sung and re-shot, and my job was to keep the satisfied but home-going audience in its seats. Canute again. They streamed past my pathetic pleas, pointing out, in the most direct way, that the last trains for Ongar and Teddington left in twenty minutes and that we should have got it right first time. It did not put me off Verdi.

Otherwise, opera is not a theatrical form I would readily seek. Maybe I have not been present at any performance that caught fire and generated that kind of heat which burns off doubt and criticism. Last night, for instance, I sat in a box, dutifully, at La Scala in Milan. I was infinitely impressed by the attendants who conveyed us thither. I was in the right geographical position to see Ricardo Muti keep a tingling hold over the orchestra. But the stage performance was barely average. I know very well that, only under the most exceptional circumstances, do you sing when you are climbing into bed. But here, in La Scala, I was looking at all the wrong things and thinking the wrong thoughts, and this dramatic form works best when somehow you are seized by the throat, or bathed in an illuminating essence, and that doesn't have to be in Rome, at Carccalla.

Lodovica Verdi, not surprisingly, likes music. She likes all Verdi but prefers the later work. The first opera she remembers is *Macbeth* at La Scala. Now she goes to the theatre, with her family, as privately as possible. Their presence is not announced. Otherwise there would be as much concentration on these privileged visitors as upon the events on the stage. When pressed a little further, the face cracks into a youthful grin.

'Pop music?'

'Yes . . . I like all strange and popular music from England. I like George Michael, and I like Duran Duran, and I listen to *them*.'

A distant roll of drums suggests that Guiseppe Verdi is begining to turn slowly in his grave. At least, that's what the purists would hear across the water meadows.

Verdi's house and gardens are set in the middle of huge golden cornfields. If you have a very flat land for a garden, and some money to play with, then water is a way of causing an elegant natural disturbance to the plane. Verdi diverted the course of a large stream, and introduced it into his wooded domain and then built little canals and ponds. This cools the hot earth and makes the vegetation luxuriant. And, although there are curious coaches full of visitors, they are not 'coach-loads', with weary feet and glazed faces. It isn't a place of pilgrimage. It's a family house – and, at the risk of repeating a running theme, they do bottle their own wine. I wonder why I am hesitant about telling you this. The reason is, of course, that it will appear that my frail barque is only comfortably afloat when it is supported upon a tide of alcohol. The Northern Protestant, however liberated, still has a watchful chapel eye cocked on the opening and closing times.

But Lodovica Verdi would think it unnatural and ill-mannered not to take us into the dark drawing-room and open a bottle of the estate's liquor. We are, after all, in Italy, where water comes in expensive bottles, or doesn't come at all.

That night, in the central square of the small neighbouring town of Busetto, was a full blown performance of *Rigoletto*. It didn't start until well after nine o'clock. People must have time to dine and to relax. The place was crowded. The performance was enchanting. The audience composed of large families, children running up and down the aisles of the scaffolding. All the local mammas brought their own chairs and cushions. The police sat on the grass and smoked. Two of the violinists in the large orchestra were music students from Liverpool. Nobody stopped the town hall clock, whose heavy medieval bell tolled the hours, chiming in utterly harmonious dissonance. God, deciding to join in the festivities, had pinned a glorious yellow cheese of a moon on to the star-velvet sky. Verdi, local lad made good, was given a rousing welcome and a thunderous farewell, and young Lodovica cheered with the rest of them.

CHAPTER
EIGHT

As you approach the heart of Tuscany, you place yourself in the greatest danger. A disease, for which there is only one desperate cure, is likely to attack you. You are most at risk in Florence. There are no notices in public places, and no discreet reminders of this peril in chemists' shops. The disease has been named 'Stendhal's Syndrome'. It attacks unsuspecting visitors. They fall over and faint, and need reviving and placing in a cool quiet room. It seems to be caused by constant exposure to excessive beauty. Some cities, when you cross the boundary, have roadside notices which say: 'Welcome to . . . You are now entering a nuclear free zone.'

There is, as yet, no local government health warning: 'Too much sensual delight can seriously damage your health.'

The unaccountably popular film of E.M. Forster's novel, *Room With A View*, has much to answer for. Florentines who pass over the Arno, by the Ponte Vecchio, on their way to pick up a Wendyburger do not really understand what all the fuss is about. I have stopped people in the gardens of the Pitti Palace and in the Piazza della Signoria to ask if they can account for the vulnerability of the English, in particular. Closely following them in this constitutional weakness are the Americans. The Japanese keep this sickness at bay by closing one eye and squinting through a camera lens with the other. They are thus protected from the furious blast of technicolour history.

'Stendhal's Syndrome' can, of course, be kept in check. You have to try to limit the possibilities of attack. To ration yourself. It is difficult unless you are devoted to sybaritic pleasure. Then it isn't. God tried to contain the spread of this contamination in 1966 when he sent a disastrous flood down from the hills into the channel of the Arno. But the natural threat to this poisonous treasure house created all kinds of curious responses. Money poured in after the water had poured out. Students came from everywhere in the world with backpacks and shovels. A Welsh sheep farmer, hearing the news on the radio in his quiet valley, jumped into his Land-Rover and drove directly to the heart of the city, to put himself at the disposal of the cleaners and restorers. Counts, dukes, communists, social democrats and Sir Harold Acton put on their wellington boots and dragged priceless artistic flotsam from the stinking mud. In the streets behind the river, even today, you can still see the foul residual plimsoll-line of oil and paint and water – a macabre tide mark.

My first visit to this city was with Lord Snowdon who took me to meet Harold Acton in 1976. Tony Snowdon's mother and step-father had known Sir Harold for many years. So I entered this pleasure garden in special private circumstances.

I had been given some confidential notes and had done some homework. But facts are one thing. They are helpful little steps and props. What had not been clearly explained was the unique charm and twinkle of this all-but Ambassador in Florence. Each year adds a cubit to Harold Acton's stature. His personal history is well documented and frequently rehearsed. An extravagant and flamboyant career at Oxford in its gaudy days and nights. His love-hate relationship with Evelyn Waugh. His fictional (though not fictitious) immortalisation in *Brideshead*. His friendships with Picasso and Gertrude Stein and the Sitwells; with all the recent heroes of a vigorous pre-war artistic explosion. Subsequently, the perfection of a highly mannered person, topped with a genteel almost exaggerated sense of hospitality. Nobody could easily recall the name of the British Ambassador at any given post-war year, but everyone knew Harold in Italy.

However much you read, and however much gossip you hear about this exotic figure in a Tuscan landscape, you are not properly prepared for the core of steel which has kept him upright, despite vigorous and illiberal attacks upon his reputation, and the harsh assaults upon his health. Nothing excites the general wrath so much as the continuing presence of a person of intelligence, culture, manners and wealth.

These days, he has become too much of a friend for me to stand back and look at him through a microscope. Even now I feel just the slightest pressure upon me to defend him – against what? Or whom? I am damned if I will. One of the principles which he has stoutly maintained in his unorthodox existence is the proper need to celebrate. His house, the Villa La Pietra, a palace, a museum and a home is a single island of celebration one mile from the city centre. La Pietra – the stone – marks a one-mile stone on the old road from Florence to Bologna. If you look in the telephone directory, he appears as Acton, Sir Harold, 120, Via Bolognese, Firenze. That is carrying modesty to exalted limits.

The garden was created by his father. It falls away from the back of the villa and is composed of terraces and green alleys, and bowers, and a small open air theatre. The footlights are manicured round box hedges. There are, maybe, two hundred fine statues forming a conclusion to a walkway, or marking the turn of a path. The Germans occupied the house during the later stages of the war. They drank the cellar dry and, for some obscure reason, chipped off all the stone private parts of the classical heroes. When Sir Harold returned, he hired the services of a sculptor who was commissioned to replace the missing members. This was in the days before the transplantation of organs became medically fashionable, and the mason had, occasionally, to be reminded that a sense of proportion would here be more seemly than a flight of the imagination.

Although Harold Acton lives alone in this huge house, he has never appeared to me to be at all lonely. This is hardly surprising if the place is constantly full of secret-service policemen. They crawl around the estate with crackling walkie-talkies. Yesterday it was Lady Bird Johnson, for whose safety the bushes had to be scoured. Tomorrow, the Prince and Princess of Wales. Next week . . . 'Ah well . . . I don't think I ought to say . . .'

I have never known what secret elixir maintains such vigour. Half the time he spends apologising.

'I am afraid that you will have to take pot luck. The cook is very capricious, don'tch'a know. And, oh dear, the butler is ga-ga, and the gardeners have had to go to a local communist party conference . . .'

Strangely enough, after all the years we have spent together in Florence, and in London, I have never used Sir Harold as a teacher. I have learned things, of course, but they were as informal crumbs from his table.

'I want you to take me to your favourite place, show me, teach me. Be my bear leader, if you will.'

No sooner said than swiftly done.

'Have you ever been up to San Miniato, on the hillside over there?'

'No.'

'Come along . . .'

If you come out of Harry's Bar on the Lungarno, the embankment that runs along the river to the Ponte Vecchio, and look across the valley up to the Pizzale Michaelangelo, you can see the bold black and white façade of the Church of San Miniato. You drive along the water and then turn to the right, across any of the bridges, and make a broad ascent out of the city centre up into the woods and hills. Here are collections of wealthy villas. Some privately contained and well-guarded behind iron grilles. Others converted to large hotels. Near the peak is a little sign to the left, indicating the Church. When you have parked the car, you need to walk up through an almost precipitous cloister. You are climbing the whole time. In the heat of the day, the sun turns the centre of Florence into a crucible. By late afternoon, the breeze at this height restores the battered senses. The view is so spectacular that unless you hold on to a wall, or a rail, the insidious Syndrome of Stendhal could well nip the unprepared, and send them reeling and keeling in astonishment.

'Don't you ever tire of this constant bombardment, Harold?'

'On the contrary, I can truthfully say that it grows upon me. The alternative, you see, is not really to be entertained at all seriously. If you tire at the sight of perfection, then you are saying to yourself that there is now something missing, something gone, from within you. This view has not changed for centuries. This place, that view, was not created by an act of nature. It is a human expression. And it is of human dimension. And, like so many places in Italy, it is a place designed for people to live in, and to work in, and to

San Miniato, Florence.

play in and, as here, to pray in.'

As always, there is one fascinating story to draw you into the place.

'Miniato was an Armenian prince, massacred on the Emperor's orders in the fourth century. He had become converted to Christianity and was causing trouble of a gentle sort. But they killed him. They beheaded him in the city. The legend is that, after his decapitation, his body searched about for his head, and found it and, in great weariness, he carried his head under his arm until he struggled here, and here he was buried, and the place became a shrine. Together with many of his brothers, who were martyrs too.

'The whole place is thick with mystery. Originally, in this side chapel was a crucifix. Florence, as you know, has been a turbulent, often murderous city. A place of fierce feuding. One young lord had to witness the death of his brother, and he swore vengeance, and he met the murderer here, at Mass, and vowed to kill him. But as he was turning away from prayer to take out his knife, he saw the head of the crucifix bowed, to indicate that charity and forgiveness were more important than blind vengeance.'

The details of this strong and graceful building are astonishing. The floor is made of a huge mosaic carpet. The Crusaders brought oriental carpets back from the East and the workmen here copied these new and original patterns. Workers were then hired from Byzantium and Palestine and encouraged to make carpets of tile and stone. The church building was started in 1018, and the pavements finished in 1200. There is a strange tabernacle built almost in front of the high altar. If it were not for the harmony of the entire building, you might almost describe it as carbuncular. But it is a heavy expression of faith and devotion. And, as time is a great healer, it is also a great binder.

In 1460, a pupil of Michaelangelo was commissioned to design a side chapel to the memory of Cardinal James of Portugal. The ceilings of this little chapel are decorated with the blue and white porcelain medallions of Della Robbia. There are exquisite pictures by minor masters of the Renaissance upon each of the three containing walls.

'I think this place is unique and, incidentally, I hear you

marvelling at the blue and white aspect of this lordly creation, but I think I ought to mention that it is, in fact, green and white. I hope you do not consider it impudent of me to point this out.'

If colour blindness or shade blindness was my only problem. Still, it brings me out of a distant country, out of another time in history, and it leaves me with one small spoonful of knowledge that, otherwise, I would not have learned. Whatever other benefits I draw from this journey, I shall, one day, be able to take someone who has never heard of the Miniato, or seen his tomb, to pass on a little of the enthusiasm and the affection I have been given by Harold Acton on this late afternoon in high summer.

'I brought Prince Charles and Princess Diana here,' Harold whispers, sitting at the back of the church, resting.

'What did they think of it?'

This question is largely redundant. It is an almost natural nosey reflex, and not asked in order to improve my understanding of this building or their taste.

'We came very early in the morning. This was the first place they visited on their trip to Florence. (They stayed, incidentally, in his house.) They were quiet. I think they were moved. Some things, you know, do not require noisy acclamation. Sometimes, it is better to sit still, and look, and that's what they did.'

★   ★   ★

One of the joys of travelling is that a mood can change with such rapidity that one is left breathless with anger, or with mirth.

In the Piazza della Signoria, in the heart of this almost my favourite city, there is virtually an open-air museum. There is the proud figure of Cosimo Medici upon his treading horse; there is the Fountain of Neptune, a recycled heavy-water display, and nearby, a plaque on the pavement indicating the spot where Savonarola was burnt – and no one dared to scoop a bucket of the bubbling fountain with which to save a life. There are also replicas of Michelangelo's David and Hercules.

The best place from which to observe this immense backcloth of Renaissance history, and the modern swill of the international tide, is in a corner café called La Rivoire. It is tremendously well-placed and very popular. You see people hovering around the chairs and tables, waiting for you to finish your coffee and go, so that they can grab a rare seat and an unparalleled view.

'David' draws all the crowds. Since it is an almost exact replica of his original, the majority of those who dip in and quickly out of this historic city believe that they have gazed upon the real thing. And who, in their right mind, would disabuse them?

'That's David, isn't it?' says one weary-footed woman, carrying a heavy bag full of leather goods and chocolates.

'David who?'

'David, you know, that statue that Michelangelo did.'

'Oh, that David!' says her distracted friend. You know that she was about to say David Steel or David Frost or David Atkinson, from Bury.

'Where?'

'There.'

Then there is a long and what one hopes is some sort of appreciative, silence. The following judgement is then de-livered.

'If that's David, I wouldn't mind having a look at Goliath.'

And these two jolly wives of Bath fall into huge shaking mirth, and dab their eyes with lace handkerchiefs, and move on to the next treasure. Where there's art, there's life. And where there's life, there's hope. Some years ago, a newly elected Mayor of Sheffield was appalled by the fact that a copy of the naked 'David' stood upon the stairway of the Town Hall. His first major exercise of power was to order a small . . . what shall we call it? . . . tailored 'cosy' to be placed over the offending parts. 'Art is art, and that's all right, but I have the Mayoress's pride to consider,' he pronounced.

There is music everywhere in this hectic city. It has become a matter of principle for entertainment to take to the streets. There are the lazy-limbed left-overs of the Sixties, strumming guitars and looking unconnected. These days, it's a touch of Graceland and a little less of the Beatles, even though all they need is love and a little money. But this is also the fierce proud heat of the Renaissance and the civic display is that which offers you some sort of consort. A consort of viols, or wind instruments, or the four-part harmony of the voice. Gabrielli and Monteverdi now sell more CDs than Dylan. And it is not unpleasurable to turn a corner and to be confronted with earnest boys and girls from Oxford singing their undergraduate hearts out, earning an honest ten thousand lire, satisfying natives and visitors, and broadening what they loosely call their education.

They are making music, at this time of the Tour, in the gardens of the Pitti Palace. The Boboli Gardens, they are called. Brunelleschi, who designed and built the Duomo, turned his later attention to this Medici Palace. The Medicis are another story, and if anyone in the right position had guts and money, in that order, they would push the Hollywood cuckoos of *Dynasty* and *Dallas* out of their pre-stressed concrete nests and plan a huge and murderously popular series around the private lives of this public family. I am available to play Lorenzo.

A part of the Boboli Gardens is a vast amphitheatre which dips down, initially, from the façade of the Pitti, and then turns upwards into a decorated hillside.

Tonight, in this open-air arena, is the first night of Purcell's *Fairy Queen*. An opera. I have had, as you know, stern reservations about opera. I have had to reorganise my thoughts. I have not been properly prepared for any of this. There are early and disturbing symptoms of Stendhal's Syndrome.

Before I move to the stage, let me try to explain the geography of the audience. Imagine, if you can, a roof top. A simple roof, which, if viewed from the side, looks like a triangle. The left incline seats the audience for part one. At the interval, you climb out of your seats, move to the peak of the roof, and then descend to the right, to occupy the same seats, but facing the other way. In part one, you have the classical Medici Palace as a back curtain. In part two, the open hillside, magically illuminated, and wonderfully explored. In more than one sense, you are on the most exciting artistic roof.

If Italy is itself a theatre, which it indisputably is, then what happens to the innocent traveller if he then enters another theatre, within the original? The answer is a mixture of intoxication and disbelief.

I don't know whether Shakespeare would have made a better impression. But when he murmured, through the chorus of *Henry V*, 'Think, when we speak of horses, That you see them printing their proud hooves i' the receiving earth,' he was, perhaps, answering the limitations of the impecunious management.

No such constraints here. Horses, cattle, carriages, carts. To be precise, sixteen horses and four oxen. There are also mechanised stages which roll on to, and away from, the landscaped stage. At the dress rehearsals, one or two of these rigid leviathans jammed their wheels, and the elegant dancers, in their late seventeenth-century costumes, toppled sideways and substituted round four-letter words for the original text. And sometimes the pilot fish, dressed in the appropriate costumes, forget to bolt the rolling stages together, as required. Then, in the middle of a quietly dramatic aria, one part of the chorus find themselves sliding elegantly back down into Florence. What do you do? Do you panic in front of the audience, or do you power up your performance and pretend that this unexpected movement is part of a planned shift, and smile, and smile, and know that you are about to hit a mountainside?

The mechanics of this masque extend into the capricious realms of hidden electronics. Everybody is equipped, initially, with a hidden personal microphone. These either work, or they don't. They depend upon temperature, and humidity. So do the loudspeakers hidden in the bosky glades. They are placed to reproduce bird song – mainly nightingales and cuckoos. These birds are, by their very nature, temperamental, and made more so by the invisible twitchings of an experienced sound engineer.

It is strongly rumoured that the dress rehearsal last night did not finish, and in some confusion, until four o'clock this morning. Then any theatrical gathering is a mushroom factory for gossip and exaggeration. Then there is the multiplying factor of Italy. Some English sense tries to prevail. Kay Lawrence supervises the dancers and Roger Norrington conducts the orchestra. They have done this kind of thing before, and around the world. Norrington and Lawrence sound like a Twenties musical double act from the Palm Court of a Grand Hotel. In fact, they are clever performers of early English music and dance. They can, and do, teach the Florentines some stylish lessons.

'Is it not, perhaps, a little vulgar?' I ask, in a half-hearted way, more concerned with the appearance than the motivation.

'No,' says Roger Norrington. 'It is the large scale which frightens you. The idea of scene changes of this size, and the mechanical miracles of people appearing out of the bodies of swans is quite authentic. In the seventeenth century there were lots of outdoor displays. People sang in bushes. And, over there, they used to have immense horse ballets. Sixty to a hundred and eighty horses, in ranks, wheeled about to music. And over here (pointing at the Pitti) they used to flood the courtyard and have pretend sea-battles. This is one of the most majestic settings in the whole of Europe.'

It is. It most certainly is. Even though, on this the first night, we have not yet reached the interval and it is twenty minutes past midnight. Who, though, is really counting?

So often, in this public arena called either Italy or the theatre, some of the best performances take place behind the scenes. There is one particularly powerful performer, flitting about the stage in a heavy velvet gown, trimmed to kill, with a head-dress which is composed of fine floating feathers. Something else attracts the eye. There is a lively edge to this performance. You know that, on the film screens and sometimes on television, certain performers, and in particular women, give a mint-fresh display of their genius. I feel that Glenda Jackson is experiencing everything for the first time, and that she is experiencing it privately, and that no one is watching or overhearing. As indeed I do with Judi Dench and Maureen Stapleton. It is some kind of innocent and mysterious surrender to the truth of things. Maybe they have worked hard to burn away all artifice. In that case, art lies unconcealed, and by 'lies', I mean what I mean.

This quality is demonstrably a part of the performance of Lesley Garrett.

'I might have known that she came from Doncaster,' he said, as yet another northern bubble bursts upon the surface of my snobbery.

Lesley Garrett is a cross between Barbara Windsor and Joan Plowright. Neither of these two companions will welcome such an arbitrary comparison; nor, for that matter, would Lesley Garrett. Though, of that, I am not at all sure.

Lesley Garrett - Pitti Palace - Florence

She has all the bounce and the vitality and bravura of the one, and all the cunning and care of the other. Then she has this frame which is currently called Garrett; and she comes from Doncaster. Tonight she has been in great trouble.

'I discovered half-way through, as no doubt you heard, or didn't more likely, that I'd lost my little tail. No tail, no voice.'

'Tail?'

'Microphone. I ran like hell for leather to try and find it. I have this mate who fiddles with me. I say "me", I mean my aerial equipment. I call him "Acoustico Paolo". And behind there it's like a cross between Covent Garden and Bertram Mills. Paolo found another aerial and pushed it down my bra . . . well, not bra, but here, there.'

Here is another radiator. Full of energy, having whisked through half a triumph and half a disaster, she is still up for air.

'We've had a fortnight to try to rehearse. And it's chaos. Utter, utter chaos. You know all the things about Italians. Oh dear me, all those little lovely things in the guide books, narrow streets, old buildings, passionate temperaments, and, you think, well it's not England, but it's nice. *Then* you have to start work with "it" and "it" drives you mad.'

Acoustico Paolo is still fiddling with Lesley's bosom. What goes up must, in some kind of way, come down. The two of them look as though they are enjoying it, though one of them looks as though they are enjoying it slightly more than the other.

'This lot,' (breezily including Paolo) 'have taken the art of upstaging to a new height. I was thinking, earlier on, that this aria's going OK. Then gradually, through the lights and the distant dimness, I began to realise that nobody – absolutely nobody – was listening to me. So I looked across this acre of a stage and saw two beautiful five-year-old children, in shiny pink leotards, little cupid's wings, there they are, playing with a monkey. I don't know where they've come from. They weren't there last night. Surprised? I was surprised. I was quite taken with them.

'Don't talk to me about Verdi and Puccini and grand dramatic themes. The Italians *all* think they are in a sit-com, day and night. Opera here is what happens in the course of any typical day – people screaming and shouting and being . . . er . . . confrontational. The only bloody difference between life and art, in this place, is me feathers on me hat.'

Intoxicated now by this energy, this boldness, this frankness, I start to audition for a part.

'You mean, throughout the length and breadth of this land, there are women singing lustily in bushes, with men's hands inside their blouses?'

'Precisely. If I were in Tesco's in the check-out queue in Doncaster, with this half an ostrich on my head, I bet they'd let me go to the front of the queue!'

I didn't want to leave Florence. I am so at home in this city. I know short cuts from this place to that. I know the best restaurant, behind the Piazza della Signoria, called 'Paolo' – not with an 'Acoustico'. I like the barman at Harry's Bar on the Lungarno, pretending to know who I am, and taking a high flyer, saying, 'It's nice to see you again', when clearly he is not altogether sure that it's your second or eleventh visit. I can follow the geography of the city, which is almost entirely to do with the long straight line of the Arno, and the opposite high hill. You know where you are. I admire the solidity and the dependability of the buildings. Merchants' houses and medieval banks. Community palaces and market places. And though the traffic thunders around the city, and the streets are jammed, there is no stalking, narrow-eyed warden waiting to slap a ticket, or clamp an innocent wheel.

The Ponte Vecchio is a boring place. It has been overtaken by the rest of the wandering, loose world. Nobody can possibly want to buy trinkets and rings and the kinds of pictures you can obtain on the railings of the north side of Hyde Park. The best place to take in the grandeur of the exterior of the bridge is from The Wendyburger on the Torrigiani. This is a serious hamburger joint with one of the world's most memorable views. The food isn't up to much. But then you know what you are buying, and it's fast and clean.

I had to face a most difficult problem here. We were in a group drinking Coca-Cola, and watching the world drift by.

'What did they say when they first declared the Ponte Vecchio open?'

A long silence, punctuated by the suck and fizz of straws in a can. Then more silence. No one has addressed themselves to the serious historical nature of this question.

'How do you mean?'

'Well . . . you know Ponte Vecchio means "Old Bridge?"'

'Yes, yes, yes . . . Go on.'

'Did someone say, on the first brand-new morning, "I now declare the Old Bridge open"?'

Whenever I leave the magnificent city of Firenze, I send home cards, picture postcards, usual messages: 'Weather fine, food v. good. Hope this finds you as it leaves me. Love from Florence, and the kiddies.'

★   ★   ★

If it is not too dangerous a claim to make at this stage, I would need to say that I could live happily, for the rest of my life, in this corner of the world. Others can bed themselves in the English contour and gentle pastureland manner of the Dordogne. Yet others may crave the instant delights and astroturf greenery of California. Some people, heaven help us all, actually enjoy living in London. Nobody, in this respect, is perfect.

Look now at Cetinale, Sovicille, near Siena. Another of the joys of Florence is that I know how to penetrate the suburbs in a swift and efficient manner and catch the autostrada, the A11 south to Tuscan countryside, south to Siena. Sovicille is an almost non-existent village even on a large-scale map, twenty minutes to the south-west of Siena. This is the expansive home of Lord Lambton, his friends and visitors (sometimes the same people) and eleven stray dogs, a white cloud of doves, the odd tractor, a holy wood, a ghost, and his own substantial dwelling.

Once you have seen Lambton's little kingdom, you don't need to ask any of the tedious questions by which he must be frequently bombarded.

What are they?

They are, in no particular order of significance, 'Why have you chosen to live in Tuscany rather than in the family seat in the North of England? Or London? Don't you miss the newspapers, the television, the rain, *Yesterday in Parliament*,

Radio 4, licensing hours and all the thousand natural shocks that a tough Briton is heir to? After all, Tuscany is such a peaceful part of God's good green earth.'

'Peaceful . . .' he muses languidly. (He is one of nature's languid musers.) 'Not sure about that. The police raped a girl here last year . . . did you read that . . . Carabinieri? Sort of gang bang . . .'

'Is it dangerous in the streets?'

'Is what dangerous?'

'Er . . . life . . . four-letter word . . . big "if" in the middle'; even I am beginning to muse langorously.

'Well, they have a game in Florence . . . just been there, haven't you? Harold said you were coming. What were we talking about?'

'Violence.'

'Dreadful. They have a game in Florence. Football. Last year they had to make a rule that you couldn't bite people's ears off. Quite comic, don't you think? What?'

I quite like any unconscious affectation, like the use of the interrogative 'What?' as a pause for breath, and a brief litmus test upon the response of the listener. Lord Lambton 'whats' often.

'One man chewed off his opponent's ear and then spat it out in the middle of the game, and then they all went on with the game.'

They say that this house, Cetinale, is haunted. There is no feel of chill, and it is difficult to believe that the presiding spirit could be malign.

'My secretary had the oddest experience. She's a very cool little girl (she is indeed), and she woke up one morning to find a heavy weight lying on top of her . . . what?'

'Er . . . (this is beginning to get a little out of hand). Er . . . when you say heavy weight, is that a heavyweight or . . . what?'

'Anyway,' he continues, disregarding this unsuitable distinction, 'I said, "Weren't you afraid?" and she said, "No", but there was this presence there, you see. There's another haunted room because the last marquis who lived here had a rather unfortunate habit. He couldn't make love, what? Couldn't, as it were, reach any kind of climax unless he strangled the love object. Throttled her. Rather unfortunate, what? So he had to take precautions. He had to have a footman in a little room next door. The footman's job was to listen, and when he thought he heard the appropriate or, as it happens, inappropriate moment approaching, he had to run in and well . . . stop it. Rather an odd job for a butler, but it was a convenient form of contraception. I think this may be what you have noticed. The room has a certain air, don't you think?'

The conversation wanders through all kinds of attractive side roads. The neighbours don't think of him as a slightly eccentric milord. They don't believe that he has true aristocratic blood. The reason is that in such a grand house no one would use big, worn, comfortable sofas. Surely, if he were a real gentleman, he would have spindly gilt chairs elegantly positioned in the drawing-room. And what about eleven stray dogs, and all those shedding hairs?

We chatted about the dreaded Stendhal Syndrome. He rechristened it Berensonitis. One day, jogging in a pony cart in Tuscany, Bernard Berenson came around a corner and his eyes fell upon the classical view. Rolling hills and the distant slim pencils of cypress. He fell forward in a faint. That's a classic symptom of the local scourge.

The laws of Italy are both curious and irritating. If you import a work or art, from your English home to your Italian villa, you have to pay an import tax which is twenty per cent of the value of the object.

'I wanted to bring in an Italian picture of an ancestor of mine who lived in this country in 1780. I thought it would be nice to have it here. When I got to the frontier, they said you've got to give us twenty per cent, and I said no, and sent it straight back. Ridiculous. They couldn't explain it. Exporting. Yes. Importing . . .'

'Do you speak reasonable Italian?'

'Not a word. Not one word.'

'I do not believe you.'

'I cannot pick up a word of any foreign language. Never been able to.'

Now, I am not so sure about the eccentricity of an expatriate lord. I am not sure about my leg being slightly pulled.

'But what happens when you break down on the motor-way, and want a drink?'

'I can't drive. And I don't drink. Does that answer your question?'

'I . . . er . . .'; I am lost.

'Do you know a Cardinal made the final alterations to this house and lived here. It's a Roman house, really, set down in Tuscany. He had a concubine and he murdered a rival, and the dead man used to come here every night and upbraid him, and it sort of got on his nerves.'

'It would.'

'So he went to ask the Pope for a confession and absolu-tion, and the Pope said, "Everything has a price," and made him turn his concubine house, see, there, up on the hill, into a monastery, and made him climb up that hill on your knees, and plant a holy wood, and fill it with penitential statues.'

By now, of course, I am having a small attack of a vari-ation of Stendhal's Syndrome. Flaubert's Fever? Proust's Poison?

There are no natural breaks in the conversation. I feel as though I am standing under Niagara Falls with a small cracked cup, trying to catch a sustaining mouthful of water, but soaked by the effort. Maybe if I take the initiative . . .

'Do you know, I am on my way to Siena. For years I've read about the Palio, and I've seen pictures, and documentar-ies and goodness knows what. But I've managed to get into, or on to, a little balcony, and I . . .'

'It happened sixteen times in the wood here.'

'It?' Is he talking about Popes and concubines and foot-men, or footballers chewing ears, or what? 'Basically, it's a horse race, stupendous. But bloody and violent. The civic authorities wised up in the late seventeenth century and they chose this place as their racecourse, out of town. They had to walk eight miles to see the race and they were tired out when they got here. I think it must be awfully difficult to be violent after an eight-mile walk in the heat . . . what?'

As my mouth gets wider in the wonder of it all, I find myself speculating about lordly possibilities. Not even ennoblement, just wealth. The combination is most subtly attractive and particularly when it is attached to talent. The talent to know that a good story is worth telling to someone else. The Wheldon Syndrome. Lord Lambton meets the Ancient Mariner, and he's the one on the left.

'I wish I could make money by telling stories', I said. I want to make a million pounds, like Jeffery Archer, so that I can buy a little house in Tuscany and withdraw from it all!'

I let this speculation float and combine, in wisps of wistfulness, with His Lordship's cigar smoke. He is thinking about this too.

'Then, why don't you do the football pools?'

And my high requiem becomes a sod.

★ ★ ★

The Palio takes place twice a year and has to be seen once in a lifetime. It is, as Lord Lambton indicated, a grand, frantic and dangerous horse race. It lasts for, maybe, three minutes. The civic authorities of this most beautiful, most unspoiled Tuscan city, lay a mixture of mat and sand around the perimeter of the Campo, the square, which lies deep in the bowl and the open heart of the perfectly preserved medieval film set.

Twice a year the city is closed to all normal traffic, and twice a year all the electric and emotional energy of proud and volatile families and, particularly, their younger male scions, is channelled into three murderous minutes. Comparisons are difficult. Imagine some remote scientist, of rare genius, evolving a system whereby he could cap the energy of the Olympics, Wembley, Wimbledon, Epsom, Liverpool, Manchester and the New York Dodgers, and funnel all this power into a small geyser which he then pumps up into this small square. It is an extreme claim to place upon the imagination of anyone who has not witnessed the spectacle. And yet, the Grand Tourist must, perforce, carry on his back, a big bag of superlatives. Mine is getting empty. I have now to scrabble about to find an adequate badge to pin on to the Palio. When John Wells dragged me, at a hare's pace, through the Pergamon Museum in East Berlin, I found myself uttering the strangest noises – noises of wonder, awe, amazement, disbelief. But they all, eventually, sounded the same and, ultimately, cumulatively meaningless. There is now little left in the backpack, and a few hundred more miles to go.

The city of Siena is divided into what we would call 'boroughs', and each 'contrada' has a horse and a hired jockey. There is one aim. To win the palm, the Palio, by almost any means. Each contrada has its lord, its mayor, its president, its boss. Each contrada has its gaudy banner. Each contrada has its local headquarters where a banquet is served on the eve of the race. On the morning of the nervous day, the chief takes his horse to the neighbourhood church, and the priest, in great solemnity, asperges the anxious beast in front of his altar. When every imaginable curse has been removed, and every conceivable blessing bestowed, and when a foreign mix of money, history, pride, tradition and

Waiting for the Palio. Siena

violence is finally prepared, there begins an extraordinary procession. Three hours of the most majestic foreplay; three-quarters of the male population of the city, and its outlying lands, dress up in authentic medieval costumes, and march with a determined and precise sloth around the Campo.

These days, all over the world, people grab a portion of their history and re-live it with some relish. I cannot speak of the Indians in Milwaukee, but I have dutifully attended wet weekends in England's north country, where pageants grind their damp way to weary inconclusion. The men are in doublet and hose. The hose, more often than not, is crinkled and unsuspendered. The shoes, normally Nike trainers, are wrapped in aluminium foil, curled up at the toes and serving no other purpose than that of a regretful disguise. A jock-strap or cod-piece would be considered effeminate. 'Look at our Ronald; he makes a grand knight,' they say, as this bespectacled and spotty youth drags his weary way around the town, pulling an unwilling horse and its load, Clothilda, with her lacquer dampened into an unattractive core. Lord Richmond betrays his suspicious lineage by a too-revealing glimpse of brown Hush Puppies.

No such embarrassing quarter measures here. Your boots have to be made of finer leather than his. His doublet and hose must be of rarer silk and satin than yours. Every man wears a wig. 'Wig' has such deceitful and unlovely connotations. Unless, that is, it makes you look like Lorenzo de Medici. Then, everybody wants to have his specially fashioned.

'How do you persuade all these people to take part?'

'How do you prevent them?' That is the considered response.

You are given enough time to admire these strutting peacocks. As soon as the horses have been blessed by the parish priest, and the jockeys have put on ridiculous little tin hats, like toy firemen, and the crowd has swirled down to the town's huge saucer, the parade begins.

Each horse is surrounded by bodyguards and stately citizens and swordbearers and halberdiers. If this weren't Italy, you would swear you were watching the opening scenes of a de Mille movie, cunningly redirected by Zeffirelli. The 'alfieri' carry the banners. Each 'contrada' has a name and a flag. I stuck my money on l'Aquila, the Eagle. Individually, the banners would look a touch vulgar, flapping from a souvenir stall. Together, in the slow majesty of the procession, they are an acceptable part of this historic tapestry.

And all the while, at a distance, or suddenly at hand, erupts a chorus – sung with a lusty medieval notation, almost like a battle hymn; each 'contrada' sings their 'Ere-we-go, Ere-we-go, Ee-I-Addio, When-you-walk-through-a-storm' anthem of encouragement. This haunting sound bristles the hair on the back of the neck. It is a strange, sophisticated and yet raucous hymn of passion.

The Sienese insist that the Palio is an event staged solely for the Sienese, and that visitors are not, of course, turned away. Yet they are not actively encouraged. Space is at a high premium. We managed to squeeze on to the balcony of an ironmonger's shop, facing sharp west. On 2 July, the sun is still climbing to an overhead position. There are eighty or ninety thousand spectators trapped in the central shell of the Campo, and thousands of others hanging off buildings and balancing on television aerials. The ironmonger's balcony is strategically placed at the first almost right-angled bend in the course. After what I suppose you would call 'jockeying' for position – all of a ten-minute scam or hype or psyche-up, as the men deal and barter and bribe and threaten – the race has begun. If you blink into the staring hot sun you will almost miss the sight of tons of sleek flesh hurtling towards you. The jockeys have no saddles. They have whips and sticks. This is life in a relentlessly fast lane. Some of them are drunk or high. As they arrive at the ironmonger's corner, they have to make the sharp turn. Some of them don't. This time two horses and their riders slapped into the wall beneath me. The wall is padded with huge mattresses, which softened the blow of the collision but didn't prevent the horses from being killed. Half-way round again and there are two or three riderless horses standing in a perplexedly sweaty way in the path of the incoming sweep.

This is a bloody, brutal and sudden explosion of sound and fury, signifying the relentless and unquestioning execution of a secular mystery.

The winner is borne in triumph, decorated, garlanded, worshipped, and led dangerously into the other quarters where bitterness and confusion fester and breed acts of drunken aggression. Hardly surprising. The Palio is the kind of event which raises all sorts of intriguing questions in the mind of the supposedly liberal traveller. It is not a blood sport, though it is bloody. The object is not to kill, though there is death. Though the winner prances about like a victorious toreador with his bull's ear, or a Scottish laird trying on the antlers of his dead stag, his eyes crossed by gallons of the 'celebration cream'.

Like all seemingly reasonable woolly liberals, I have all the right questions and none of the answers.

I wish I had had the right answers when I was arrested by the police the next morning. Large parts of this warren-like city are closed off to traffic. Some streets are too narrow for a motor car. Others have a daunting habit of suddenly developing steps in the middle, and you can only manoeuvre these if you are making a television commercial and you have been trained as a stunt driver.

I was making a tour of the town, noting with peevish pride that they have a litter problem consequent upon the previous big day (so much for grandiose historical pensées), when I heard the sound of sirens. Italy, however beautiful a country, is noisy. There is always a background thrum of people. There is a confusing bombardment of traffic. Often, in an operatic vein, there is thunder. And when God doesn't oblige with celestial pyrotechnics, they light their own fireworks.

I entered a quiet street and drove idly towards a side square, when, of a sudden, I heard the scream of police sirens.

'Some poor devil in trouble . . .'

The police motorbikes came behind me, drove past, did a skid turn across my path, dismounted and started the slow menacing walk to my car.

I have seen this sort of thing in movies. The cops wearing dark glasses, guns at the waist, clean laundered blue shirts, boots, smart cap pulled threateningly low. I know how they behave but I had never imagined I would have to play the victim's role.

'Senso unico!' the leader hissed.

I know that means 'one way street', and it did not need half an hour at a sophisticated computer for me to realise, at that moment, that all the cars were facing the other way. Even if I had known the Italian for, 'But I'm only going one way', I think that the combination of guns and sunglasses would have given me reasonable pause for thought.

It was an 'On the Spot' fine. I couldn't understand much of what was being said and, of course, I began to panic at the mention of thirty-seven-and-a-half thousand lire. In this kind of criminal crisis, you do not automatically divide by whatever it is.

'No, I don't have proof of identity.'

'No, I don't have my driving licence with me.'

'No, my passport is in my hotel bedroom.'

'No, I cannot remember the name of the hotel.'

'Yes, of course, I will surrender these documents to you if I can find my wretched way back to the hotel.'

Some people would think that the apogee of the Grand Tour would have been reached by the accompaniment of two police outriders, sirens screaming, lights flashing, through the historic city of Siena! Who can that be? bystanders would ask, in their curiosity about a visiting celebrity. And fat black-bombazined Italian mamas would stand agape at this Tamburlaine-type progress through their city.

'Ecco . . . the portly, balding British ex-chat show host upon his way to another glittering rendezvous!'

When we got back to the hotel, and exchanged documents, and the carabinieri seemed satisfied, I noticed, from the corner of one alert eye, that the chief policeman had suddenly become aware of the camera. The odd straightening of the tie, removing of the peaked cap to straighten the hair.

'Is this television?'

'Well . . . sort of . . .' Again, one simply could not engage upon the whole philosophy of the Grand Tour.

'When you show?'

'Oh, next year, or some time . . .'

'I have friends in England. You give me times and dates

and they will see me and like me.' By now he was pushing me out of the way and starting to behave like an actor playing the part of a policeman.

'Please may I have my licence and passport back?'

'You have him when I am ready!'

And off we go again into the exaggerated dramatics of Sienese street theatre. And would this be the right moment, do you think, to say to the macho prosecutor, in English, 'Pray do not delay me on account of I have an audience with the Pope of Rome'?

I think, perhaps, not.

CHAPTER
NINE

The Palio marks two nights and a day when the city of Siena is frozen in a medieval attitude. A lot of people, visitors included, emerge from this warp with something which could loosely be described as the 'cultural bends'. You come back up into the real world too quickly. Your head is a-dizzy with the battering of delights, and your mouth is parched by the wine of the victorious and the consolatory drownings of the defeated. That, and the police behaving like Latin equivalents of the Beaux Gendarmes.

This Tour is now beginning to accelerate a little beyond my normal northern control. It is, with immense relief, that I fall across Christopher Scaife. I had talked to lots of people about the journey before I set off. Some advice was sound, and a lot of it ludicrous. I tried to build in 'breathing holes', time for a sit-down and whatever is the Italian for putting your feet up. So far these periods have come stealing up behind me, unplanned, and have largely been concerned with the peacefulness which radiates from a religious order. And that has been the calming and hospitable house of the Benedictines.

Christopher Scaife belongs to no known order, but he is a man of quite astonishing joy, and he is skilled at the communicating of simple pleasure.

He is now in his mid-eighties. He is extremely frail and

almost blind. He broke a hip in a fall almost a year ago and
has the utmost difficulty in moving. He lives in a tiny farm-
house, which was probably a barn, standing on one side of a
courtyard where there is a lemon tree, a fig tree and a lilac
bush. Just across the courtyard (which is almost too grand a
word) is another small barn which he made into a studio
some years ago. The main room is on the top floor and you
have to climb wooden steps which have rotted, and you can't
use the handrail, because that moves disconcertingly with
you. Since his fall, he hasn't been into the studio, but he
insisted, when we arrived, that he should be made to move
out of the one house, down the stairs, across the yard and up
to the other.

This operation was organised by all willing hands, including Renato and Christina (a sort of male watchdog and a
fussy Italian hen), who come to him every day, squeeze the
lemons, make the bed, bring a little pasta and, occasionally, a
newspaper.

You would think that moving such a delicate wisp of a
body would require a certain solemnity and, at least, invoke
some strong railing against whichever God has been responsible for the infirmity and indignity of age. Not so.

'I can't think why you don't just roll me. Look, I am bent
like a hoop. If you were children, you could just bowl me
along the ground. But I must move. Haven't been out of
here for eight or nine months. You must all have wine before
we start to engineer this exercise.'

Christopher Scaife won the coveted Newdigate Prize for
Poetry at Oxford, when he was a handsome young undergraduate over sixty years ago. There was the prospect of a
bright future held, then, before him. He taught in various
universities, Beirut, Cairo, Teheran – constantly moving in
the Middle East. And he has continued to write poetry and,
which is even bolder, made damn sure that it was published
by paying for it, privately, from his own insubstantial
pocket.

'Are you a good writer?' I asked him, too cheekily, but
comfortable in the knowledge that this man is too happy a
creature, malgré tout, to be offended.

'I think so; yes. Let me quote our mutual friend Nevill

Coghill.' (Coghill was my own tutor in Oxford.) '"Dear Christopher," he would say, "a good poet but always a minor one." And I accept his judgement. I'm pleased by what I have written, and, don't tell anyone this, proud of some of it.'

'I don't think I've ever seen a Newdigate Prize Winner before,' I said.

'Well. I'll tell you one thing. I certainly did not look like this when I won. Things sort of collapse and drop off when you get older. Look at my hair. People say I should have it all cut off and not comb these wretched little strands over my dome of a morning. I'm going to have it cut off. What's the use of fiddling?' And all this with a twinkle and the slightest feeling that a leg may be in the process of being pulled.

He says he's been there for life. When you look about you, you can see why. He can't see properly the clear-edged view of the Umbrian hills, and those tall dark cypress trees which are so distinctive a feature of this golden landscape.

'But, dear boy, I can smell it all. It's heaven fresh each morning and lasts well into my night. I'll tell you something interesting. I'm an Anglican but I have permission to take the Eucharist in the local church, and I've got permission to be buried there too. I don't want any of that burning business. I don't want my ashes to be put in a little box and pushed into a pigeon hole in a church wall. What I want is to nourish the earth. Good heavens, I've had enough splendid salads in this little house. The least I can do is to fertilise the earth.'

We then hum a little of 'Ilkley Moor Bah t'at', about worms eating thee, and the simple cycle of putting back what you got out.

When Scaife says that he has enjoyed living in the Garden of Eden, you know that he is making no deep, mystical, religious claim. He's talking about sunflowers and melons and the mystical magnetism of this part of the earth which, so far on the travels, I have not managed to analyse satisfactorily. Sometimes, I am too aware that to define is to destroy.

'If I had died without seeing Italy,' I ventured at the end of our meeting, 'what would I have missed?'

Christopher Scaife sighed a little, and then put his glass into the nearly blind eye, scanned me for a moment and replied, 'One hell of a lot. But then, of course, Italy would have missed almost as much, too!'

And we laughed, and we hoisted him back to his sofa in the cluttered sitting-room, where everything is at hand's reach.

'Put me on my rubber cushion. That's my latest indulgence. I've just published another book of poetry. Give me a pen. I'll sign it while Renato pours you another glass from the big barrel in the cellar. Make sure you come back. Anytime. Anybody. Liberty Hall, this. Best day I've had for a long time. Bloody awful row yesterday with these two Italians who help me. They wanted me to wear a suit for you. I said I'm not wearing any suit in this heat. I wear jeans. I think I'm the only 250-year-old man who wears jeans. You should have been here to witness the row. I'm glad I hung on to my jeans. Have I said it's the best day I've had for years?'

I took my regretful leave. It should be abundantly clear, working again on the principle that there are only 'drains' and 'radiators' in this world, that I had been considerably, almost extravagantly, warmed by this beautiful man's presence.

★   ★   ★

The drains were waiting in Perugia. Driving into this grand city which, like so many others, keeps its architectural dignity and treasure intact at the top of a guarded hill, I saw many signs announcing a Pop Festival. Coach-loads of young men and women were arriving. It was Sunday afternoon. Hitch-hikers along the roadsides. Scruffy urchins from Rome and Arezzo. Sophisticated open car-loads of the fashionable rich. All heading into Perugia to hear Sting perform at an open-air concert that evening. Sting (a.k.a. Gordon Sumner, bright lad from Newcastle-upon-Tyne) is big in Europe. Yet again the twentieth-century manifestation of a new hero. We've talked of fashion designers and chefs. We haven't yet considered the pop star. And Sting is big.

People like this travel with an enormous retinue of attendants. Their men look permanently worried and harassed, and use walkie-talkies sometimes in order to let other people see that they are using them.

'Checking. Just checking. Over. Out.'

There is no message, except the signals which go clearly to lesser mortals. Great Italian princes, when they made their progresses from one palazzo to another, must have had similar guards. Minders they are now called, ready to deliver a hot knuckle butty if their icon seems threatened. The women, on the other hand, do not seem to have any visible rôle. They have hair which has cost millions of lire to fashion into the appearance of a rough dish mop. They don't speak. If they have anything to say, they say it when I'm not there, which is perhaps just as well. They wear a lot of leather, and the current skirt-length is roughly the approximate of a pelmet. In the olden days, they would have been carried on palanquins, and worn elaborate head-dresses, and held some proper court. I am not quite sure what they are now for, although I am not quite sure that I'm not quite sure, if you see what I mean.

The object around which these glittering and silent satellites revolve, Sting, the Star, remains largely unmoved. In the central hotel there is a balcony and we walk out of the room to look at the view and smell the air. There's a crowd gathering below. One of his henchmen looks down and says, dismissively, 'Creeps.' Sting waves. One does not know whether the sentiment is echoed or rejected.

'I often see the same faces, peeping up at me, in places like this, and at concerts. The same faces in Melbourne and in Zürich. It's madness. I often wonder what they are doing with the rest of their lives. I'm getting on with life. Why aren't they getting on with theirs?'

'Because they're getting on, or off, with yours!'

Sting scratches his head. The crowds applaud.

'Perugia is a great city,' he continues. 'The Pope built a city underneath this in an inner protective fortress . . . to make it doubly safe.'

'How do you know all this?'

'I read it in the hotel lobby this morning.'

'When you move with this great brigade, and a big band, and security, and the hermetic cocoon of wealth, how ever do you get to know the heart of a place?'

'Well, I don't ride around in a limousine. I walk around the streets and I demand that people behave sensibly. If you start running around with sunglasses on, in armoured cars, and bodyguards, then people get hysterical. I don't want to live like that. That's not freedom. It's a nightmare.'

He is basically a sensible and likeable man, and I believed what he was saying even though there was enough distracting evidence around him to deny this simplistic philosophy. He was born and brought up a Catholic, and glad of it, since it gave him something to react against, but he would not want to be Pope. His retinue behave as though they were in attendance upon the Pontiff, but Sting said, quite categorically, that he entertained no such ambitions.

'The colours wouldn't suit me,' he winks.

I went to the evening's concert. We had to queue for an hour to get even to a semi-royal enclosure. The crowd was colourful and good-natured. The walkie-talkie boys were in their element being, for one hour, able to scream and chatter, with the attendant radio and television crews, forcing people behind barriers, clearing a Red Sea path for Sting to amble through on his way to the stage and to the acclaim of the crowd.

The concert never caught fire. It was energetic and well organised, but someone forgot to press the button marked 'Ignition'. I sat on a bench, high up in the stadium, for a brief period of meditation. What would compare with this kind of hugely popular performance in the days when my man was making his original journey? Nothing that I have read or been told of approximates to the well-rehearsed commercial caravan on its roll through Europe. There must have been eighteenth-century equivalents of the T-shirt. There must, indeed, have been transient heroes. But they would have been contained locally. Nevertheless, razzmattaz is not a quantifiable outburst. Maybe a young man twanging the strings of his lute in the warm square of Perugia would have produced the same lip-quivering hysteria amongst the scarlet young faces of the town virgins. And when one of them, all of a sexual quiver, asked for his signature, his arrogant mate might have mouthed the local dialect for 'creep'.

★   ★   ★

In the past four days, I have sat with, and talked to, four

people who live lives of great contrast. An English lord, living in luxury in a beautiful villa outside Siena; a pop star, an idol, incarcerated in a large hotel and not able to see the sun because of the shade of his bodyguards; an English writer living in almost Franciscan modesty in a farmyard; and now, today, I have been invited into the Monastery of St Francis himself, in his home town of Assisi, to meet Father Max, who is the current gentle senior in this establishment.

One's moral, philosophical and physical senses are under an enormous bombardment. Father Max yet again points the way to sanity, if not to salvation. (At least, not to mine.) I have sailed rather haughtily through life so far believing that to devote your life to an order, be it Franciscan as here, or Benedictine, with Sister Scholastica in Germany, was somehow a compound of selfishness and an inability to face the harsh realities of this wicked world. Whatever else I have achieved on this journey, at least I have made a significant re-assessment of that glib judgement.

I used to believe that it was something to do with clothes. If you wore a monk's habit, or if she was wearing the sombre black of her order, then somehow you were removed, elevated, spiritualised, translated. I can still remember the first time I saw a priest smoking a cigarette and drinking a glass of beer. The daring! The outrage! Maybe, too, holiness descends upon a person if they are fortunate enough to live on a private island, like Scholastica, or here, high on the walls of Assisi, in a thirteenth-century building with frescoes and courtyards and fountains, and the Franciscan symbols of swallows wheeling in the evening air, and doves cooing, and the rich and complicated texture of Vespers offering some kind of acceptable ecclesiastical muzak.

'What about Moss Side?' I asked, emboldened by the big gulps of undiluted spirituality.

'What is Moss Side?'

'Moss Side is in Manchester, near to the place where I work. It's ugly. It's as far away as you could imagine from here, in feeling, that is. I just wonder how you would try to find peace, or an inner calm, or God, or whatever you call it, in an unhappy place like that?

'You are being very presumptuous, very naive,' the

smiling Father replied. 'Any kind of peace or calm, you carry with you. You take it there. That's a little about St Francis. He was rich, you know. When he was using his father's money to eat and drink lavishly with his friends, his father made no complaint. When he threw all that away, gave his clothes away, too, sold everything and walked out into the countryside, here, his father disowned him. But he carried his faith unclothed and inside. He didn't have any intention to start an order, to form an order of brothers. This city, in the walls that is, still has a population of only twelve hundred people. The rest are pilgrims coming to honour Francis. It all comes from inside, you know. In Moss Side, it would come from inside. I know these things. I travel a lot. This year I have been to Sweden, and to Finland and to Japan, and to England.'

'You seem to me to be an ecclesiastical Grand Tourist.'

'I am. I am. But strange things happen to those who make journeys.'

'Like what?' I ask, knowing full well that strange things have occupied my journey thus far.

'I was invited to take a cup of tea with the Archbishop of Canterbury at Lambeth Palace. So I went on 15 June at three o'clock in the afternoon and there was not a cup of tea. But instead he was waiting for me with a medal, the Cross of St Augustine. For my work with ecology, and the Duke of Edinburgh, here in Assisi.'

'Did you have tea after that?'

'We had tea after that, thank you.'

Father Max told me lots of extraordinary stories. About pilgrimages, for example, upon which he had to walk for thirty miles barefoot.

'In penance?'

'No. The straps of my sandals broke.'

Prince Charles who in many ways is a secret and some-times accidental Grand Tourist, took a deep breath when Father Max showed him the stupendous frescoes in the Upper Basilica at Assisi. This is artistic bravery of size and a conception one rarely meets outside the Vatican or some great cathedral. Giotto was commissioned to paint twenty-eight scenes from the life of Francis. He worked with his scaffolding, and his tetchy pupils, between 1296 and 1304. The result is breathtaking.

Prince Charles, suitably stunned, gazed at these compositions of powerful irregularity, with mad perspectives, and said to Father Max: 'If you had had a Reformation, like we had, they would have had this lot off the walls in no time!'

Next door to the monastery and the basilicas is an old-fashioned comfortable hotel called The Subasio. The windows of my room opened on to a little balcony. When I was going to bed that night, after drinking a coffee and a sambucca with the resident PRM (Public Relations Monk), I opened the windows and saw the entire valley below, bathed in summer moonlight, and every window of the monastery cells darkened by the strict curfew of the order. I did not say my prayers. I am currently prayerless, having expended amounts of the wind and air of enthusiasm and approval upon all that I have privately witnessed today. If I had prayed, I would have said, 'Thank God they are all safely enclosed in their cells, and thank God I am comfortably stowed in this, my room, with a telephone, and an electric light that I can switch on and off without guilt or the possibility of penance.' There is no moral judgement here implied. They are quite probably happier and more at ease with the world. This is not my road.

Rome, yes. Damascus, no!

★　　★　　★

It took two sweating, furious and frustrating hours to drive from Rome's boundary to the Hilton Hotel. Backwards and forwards and in a loop, and ending in a railway yard, with much cursing and little of the brotherly love of St Francis with which I have been so recently infused. Eventually a taxi driver guided me up the Monte Mario and delivered me to the sybaritic pleasures of this portion of the new world set down so dramatically in the heart of the old.

Let us dispose of criticism and the up-throwing of indignant hands. The Rome Hilton? Are you supposed to be a Grand Tourist? Don't you think you should have stayed in a little albergo, a modest pensione at the foot of the Spanish

Steps in the shade of the Keats-Shelley House?

No. Thank you.

I don't find Rome a comfortable or attractive city. I can't really tell where I am. People say that it is a pleasant conglomeration of villages, each with a piazza, a church, a local restaurant and a character of its own. The problem is that the River Tiber curves at random through the city and, since I tend to use a river as a point of location and direction, I am consequently lost most of the time.

The temperature is throbbing at almost one hundred degrees Fahrenheit. It is mid-August. The city is packed with tourists (of whom, naturally, I am one) and with pilgrims. Tomorrow I am going to a Papal Audience in the Vatican. Meanwhile my energies are exhausted, and I am looking forward to a strong shower, a large comfortable bed and the full blast of air-conditioning.

The view from my balcony is all embracing. The hotel sits upon the top of one of Rome's surrounding hills. One side of the hotel looks directly upon a large television transmitter. That is uninspiring and must cause dreadful annoyance to the travellers who are assigned to that side. My side looks upon the boiling crucible of the city centre, and at the mildly disappointing dome of St Peter's, not so impressive as the Duomo in Florence. In fact, after the happy times and excitements of Florence, Rome is, frankly, a let-down.

However, refreshed by the rest of a cool air-conditioned night, and the invigorating force of a shower for which one had almost to chain the ankles to the bath in order not to be knocked down by the Niagara, I took a glass of fresh orange juice out onto the balcony just at that moment when the still air was filled with a great noise. It was eight o'clock and, in from his summer palace at Castel Gandolfo, the Pope's helicopter was lowering him from the blue sky into the Vatican gardens. This was a strange and rather moving vision. This is how I had hoped one or two precious, or peculiar, moments of the Tour might manifest themselves. The helicopter is a romantic machine – private and clever, reaching into secret gardens, whisking the powerful and the protected up and away, a machine which has certain God-like properties, and is also used by James Bond.

The Pope gives an Audience every Wednesday morning at half-past ten. The Audience chamber is rather like a garish aircraft hangar. The crowd behaves as if it were a part of a warm-up for a Cup Final. There is a great deal of singing and banner-waving. The noise level is high. The stewards are dressed in morning coats. Two or three Cardinals float around the Pope's throne. There are rigid and unblinking Swiss Guards flanking the doors through which the Pope will arrive. There are others, equally erect and immobile, around the throne. There are twelve of us (in no apostolic order) sitting on the front row of the Audience chamber. Each one of us is sponsored or escorted by an approximate guardian from the Vatican staff. I am being shepherded by a Monsignor from the English College. There is plenty to attract the attention as we wait for the arrival of the Holy Father. There are even people cruising around with walkie-talkies, reminding me unfavourably of the Sting concert in Perugia.

The expectation rises, with the approach of the hour. So does the noise. Then, suddenly, the Pope strides out of a side door, his arms held wide in greeting, and the Audience chamber explodes. The cheering lasts for maybe all of three minutes and, had he not made it perfectly clear that enough was then enough, would probably have gone on for three hours.

His throne is too big for him. He moves around restlessly upon it. He didn't seem at all relaxed or happy. Two servers swing a microphone in and up to his face for a prayer of greeting, and then swing it back for him to listen to the messages from the crowds. Each country there represented has a sponsoring Cardinal who goes through an exhausting list of separate visitors. 'The Clare Junior High School from Haybury, Wisconsin' . . . shrieks, and all the waves and flappings of hysterical drum-majorettes. The Pope put his right hand to his forehead and closed his eyes. This job isn't all High Masses and Monteverdi and visits to S. America. Part of his duty, and a happy part too, is to sit here and smile at all the world. Then he offers another prayer in the language of the country he is blessing. This morning there were seven translations.

He has, of course, a magnetic presence. Anyone who is the object of such worship and hysteria assumes a strange kind of other-worldliness, a sort of film-star aura. We know enough small personal details about him to add another layer to the appeal. Private mountain climbs. Ski-ing. Writing poetry. And the extraordinary canonisation that is bestowed upon anyone in high office whose life is threatened by an assassin's bullet.

I stared at the Pope for one and a half hours and I became obsessed by his shoes. When he is sitting firmly, and in a severe upright position, his feet hardly touch the ground. But his shoes were extraordinary. They were brown, made of what seemed to be cheap leather, with rubber soles which had obviously been through puddles and not dried properly. They were turned up at the ends, like the shoes we wore at school. I had expected the Shoes of the Fisherman to be made of finely tooled leather like the medieval slippers worn by the young men in the Sienese Palio. These were well-used True-form.

When the official part of the ceremony was finished, His Holiness bounded out of the throne and into the aisles of the hall, moving quickly and shaking every offered hand. There were doors opened to the street. I was amazed at the lack of

any too obvious security.

Finally, he came to the front row, and, in turn, I was presented by my Monsignor. No cameras, please. No microphones was the order. We shook hands. His grip is firm and his eyes fix you and he has an engaging smile. The conversation was stilted. We talked of tourists of whom, I understood, he had seen quite enough that morning, thank you. He holds your hand whilst he is talking and it was, therefore, possible to observe that he wore only one cuff-link. His cuffs, on the other arm, were free-flapping. He gave me his blessing, and I bowed in gratitude. And yet, in some undecided and inexplicable way, it was not the high point I had expected it to be.

I have wondered to myself since, why I was so intrigued by shoes and cuff-links, and not infused by a higher spiritualism. I felt more comfort and more of the satisfying heat of real faith in Chiemsee and Assisi. I was more impressed by the little Breughel in Liechtenstein than by the grand panoply of the Vatican.

I did not, however, leave the Vatican without one special thrill. Later that afternoon, I went to meet a gentle Irishman called Father Boyle, who is the Keeper of the Vatican's Private Library. His real title is 'The Prefect'.

'The job goes back to 1450 and I go back just two years.'

That particular week, a gift of letters and diaries belonging to an Italian aviator of the mid-1920s had been offered to, and accepted by, the collection. There is an awful lot of documentation about balloons and early flying machines, and one wonders, idly, what all this is doing in the Vatican Archives. The Prefect explains, in his customary quiet way, that it is his duty to accept what is reasonably offered and then to allow history to make a longer term judgement. Virgil and the Gutenberg Bible, he admits, are probably going to be of greater interest to future scholars – they are here, locked in that room, there – but he is not in the business of reading historical runes.

To his small desk, he brings a vellum-bound collection of letters from Henry VIII to Anne Boleyn. He puts the book on a little lectern, places his spectacles upon his nose and starts to examine the text.

'I'll go rather slowly, if you don't mind. Now, this is one that Henry writes to Anne to tell her that there are hopes of a divorce on the way. The legate has arrived from Paris, and he throws in a little bit of his love with it. Normally, these letters begin with little terms of endearment like "darling", or "my mistress". This one just starts off straight.'

And he begins to read, following the small calligraphy with his forefinger.

'The reasonable requests of your last letter, with the pleasure also that I take to know them true, causes me to send you now this news. The legate, which we most desire, arrived at Paris, on Sunday or Monday last past. So that I trust that by next Monday to hear of his arrival in Calais. And then, I trust to enjoy that which I have so long longed for, to God's pleasure and our both comforts.

'No more to you, at this present, my own darling, for lack of time. But that I would you were in mine arms or I in thine, for I think it is long since I kissed you.

'Written after the killing of a hart, at eleven of the clock and minding, with God's grace, to kill another tomorrow. Now written by the hand of him which I heartily trust shall be yours. Henry Rex.'

This reading clearly pleases The Prefect as much as it pleases me. The letters are charming. Composed, almost like prose poems. Father Boyle rightly says that they betray none of the heavy exasperation of this mad-head monarch who stands astride, in the picture of one's historical eye, with his hands on his hips, a prominent garter and well-made shoes.

Several letters end in deliberately designed signatures, little pictures with HR intertwined and the initials AB contained in a tiny heart. Infinite care and an eye for proportion and detail from someone whom you might naturally expect to have ordered a Tudor Kissogram.

All my life, I realise as I take farewells of Father Boyle and his treasures, all my life I have been obsessed by teaching and by learning. The one is as stimulating as the other, and today I have been again a willing and excited pupil. As I drive back to the Hilton, which Henry VIII would have enjoyed, I am more kindly disposed to this foreign city.

CHAPTER
TEN

If you have followed me thus far, you will now know and understand two things. The first is that, in the natural dynamic of the journey, I am much more in love with Italy than with any other part of the travels. The second is that I am more comfortable and more confident when I am being led and guided by someone who wants to communicate an enthusiasm. None of this has to be cosmic. I don't look for the large lessons of history, but I can be moved by the design of a garden or the eccentricity of a tomb. I value the experience in human terms when I think of Armani's old rocking horse standing in his new sitting-room. The Pope's curled-up shoes tell me more about the man than a whole history of the Papacy.

Before I leave this Eternally noisy city, I have an appointment with Franco Zeffirelli. He has taught me much about the swirl and bite of Italian life in his films. Great swags of washing hanging in the laundry in the house of the Capulets, in his rich *Romeo and Juliet*. His pictures breathe and smell of all the antique richness of the northern Italian city-states. Even the least successful of his historical movies, *Brother Sun and Sister Moon*, about the early life of St Francis, has stamped such strong images of this country upon me. I don't even know whether any of Zeffirelli's films have been lodged in the Vatican Archive. If they haven't, they should be.

It doesn't take him long to understand what it is I am look-ing for. But there is an attractively perverse streak in him. We were sitting in his cool garden, in a part of Rome that reminded me strongly of Surbiton, and I was telling him of the Vatican Archive and all the little treasures I had seen and handled. After two or three of his generous glasses of a forti-fying liquid, I made my, by now, customary declaration of appreciation for this dazzling country – Rome notwith-standing. How I wanted two acres and an old barn, and an olive tree, and some fresh figs, and all the attendant nonsense of the flush of first love.

'What's wrong with England?' he enquires.

I rush headlong into the litany of complaints about English rain and peevishness and prurience and licensing laws. All this is dismissed.

'I owe a lot to England,' he says, 'and to Scotland. My nanny was Scottish and she taught me, in Florence, as a child. Later on, when the British came to liberate us, I crossed the line to join the Eighth Army – the First Battalion of the Scots Guards.'

All this seems mightily incongruous.

'They changed me with ivory soap. They cut my hair, sheared me, cut me like a goat. In two hours, with a kilt, I became a perfect – how you say? Celt!'

All this seems mightily incongruous too. I had not been prepared for such a lesson, which continued, at some length, with a paean of praise in favour of the English countryside. At this moment I heard what sounded like English dogs barking. Unqualified praise in favour of the English countryside, the gentleness of the English climate which puts the rose upon the cheek, the soft rain, the sense of history. This latter is absurd. Especially from someone called Zeffirelli, sitting here in his Roman garden. What need of a sense of history when one is sitting in the presence of it?

The odd thing about this encounter is that a Roman villa looking like the house of a venerable patrician is just inside the ring road. One had expected something rather grand on a hill, with porticos and fountains and peacocks. Instead of which there is an iron gate, electronically controlled, a busy bee of a housekeeper, and the near hum of fast cars racing round the city. The dogs were barking in one corner of the grounds.

'They've probably found a fox,' Zeffirelli says.

'A fox? In the middle of Rome?'

'Yes. This is just inside the ring road, this place, and there is a law here, one of the few good laws in Italy, which says that you cannot shoot or hunt any wildlife inside that ring. So here are rare birds back again. Nobody pinging . . . do you say pinging? . . . and here are rabbits and foxes. Now we have vipers and small falcons.'

Zeffirelli begins to sound like St Francis. Brother Sun.

'Listen to the call of the cricket. She doesn't think about the winter. The ant, though, works through the summer to store for the winter. When winter comes the cricket is dying of hunger and begs the ant, saying, "Please give me something to eat." The ant says, "You should have sung less during the summer," and slams the door. What were we talking about?'

Well! I don't really know by this time, Signor Zeffirelli, I don't really know. I thought I had started to muse about affluence and industry but then he began to tell me a fable. And he is an excellent teller of tales, and I have mentioned before, in this journal, that I am bewitched by a well-told story.

I had suggested that the English had the wrong idea about the Italians. We would snigger dismissively and say that there had been thirty-five governments since the war, and no one really knew what they were doing, and the electricity doesn't work, and people rather like lying around in the sunshine and drinking and pinching ladies' bottoms.

'Some of that is true. A leetle bit. Bottoms, yes. But people like to make money. They get up early in the morning, with the sun. They sit in the same sun after a lunch. It is sensible. Then they go to work until the evening. They don't sit inside watching television in rain. Or, if they watch, the women do knitting and sewing. It is true that they don't want you to think that they work all the time. They hide that. But they like money. We like the money. I like money too.'

'So do I.'

Zeffirelli has made a lot of money, and spent a lot too. He has a sumptuous property at Positano on the coast, south of Naples. He holds a kind of court there. Dinner in the evenings is not taken until very late, until, indeed, he is ready. People are invited for short or long stays. If you happen to be called Olivier, it is a comfortable and convenient place in which to rehearse a part. Some years ago Zeffirelli was asked to direct a series of da Fillipo plays at the National Theatre. Olivier, as the rest of the world knows, has to have every detail right. He was to play the part of an old Neapolitan, so he went to the south of Italy to watch people walk, and talk and argue and barter and make love.

'It wasn't easy,' says Zeffirelli, 'even for Larry who is very quick in learning tricks. It took a long time. He talked a lot with the people. He watched my butler, my cook, everybody. He started with them. I remember seeing him hiding away and trying to remember what the language of the hands meant, and he got it very clear, very right. Made little drawings like . . . what you say . . . semaphore? The hands are almost entirely an expression of your feelings, you know!'

I remembered Ruth Donadoni's lessons in Bergamo. She sent me off with a preliminary exercise in hand language. It has proved useful all the way down the leg of Italy and, even here, in Zeffirelli's garden, I can easily understand what he was teaching Olivier.

'What do you want . . . Leave me alone . . . Go away . . . Come back . . . Heaven help me . . . I kill you. I keeel you!'

And everything done by hand, even the killing.

'You are going to Naples, no?'

'Yes.'

'Never make this sign.' He makes the shape of horns with his fingers, and puts them on his head.

'I don't think I will have occasion to do that.'

'You will be keeled if you do. It means that you say other men enjoying my wife.'

Well into the swing of this conversation by now, I ventured the idea that the British did not make full use of their hands. Rather, they were kept stiffly to the side – except when saluting the flag at sundown.

'You use hair.'

'Hair?'

'Mrs Thatcher, great woman, great presence, she says it all in her hair.'

There are moments, and this was one, where you have to make a swift political and diplomatic decision. Nothing to do with the Prime Minister, you understand, but whether you should pursue such strange by-ways of conversation. Would it not, perhaps, settle things more quietly if one nodded in agreement without the least possible idea of his meaning? Except that I knew what he meant but I didn't want him to pick out each strand of Mama Tatcha's coiffure and analyse its significance.

'Two things, sir,' I said. 'I am bound for Naples and would welcome any advice you could offer to a passing traveller. Before that, what should I see, upon your recommendation, in Rome?'

'Naples first,' he replied. 'Know that it is dominated, in every sense, by Vesuvius. So that everyone in Napoli is a survivor. At every step you could be killed. Life is cheaper. They don't really know why they are there. Behind the love, behind the money . . . and there is little distinction between the two . . . beyond imagination and beyond the invention . . . and there is much evidence of both, there is the memory of the terrible tragedy of Pompeii. It is in the mind, the heart, the bloodstream. Your life can burn up in a minute!'

'Aren't you being rather dramatic about this?'

'No. No. That mountain has not smoked properly for forty years. Can you imagine this? All the people feel that there is a hard plug on the top of the volcano and, inside, this tremendous natural pressure ready to blow, ready to go. They are haunted by it. Haunted. Haunted. (Lots of gesticulation, now, in this most agitated of performances.)

'It conditions art, music, literature, philosophy. And that is my firm belief about Naples. And you love it or you hate it much. And there is nothing – No Thing – in between. But Rome? Do you know the Gardens of the . . .?'

'Finzi Contini?'

'Wait. Wait . . . The Villa d'Este?'

'No.'

'Put that glass down. Get into your car and go to the Villa d'Este. You will like it. There is much to cool and satisfy.'

Taste, at the end of a hot day, is taste. What excites or satisfies me, may not do the same for you, yet it is a subject to be explored, and even to be taught by example. If Zeffirelli tells me to go to the Villa d'Este, I am not likely to ignore his injunction. If God suddenly descended in a light cloud and said to me that, for a day, I could be anyone I wanted, I would choose to be Zeffirelli. If the name itself isn't enough, the achievements certainly are, and if they weren't, then the persuasive use of hands and language would lead me to the same conclusion.

★　　★　　★

The Gardens of the Villa d'Este were cooler and more satisfying than Zeffirelli had suggested. Water, water everywhere, and plenty of it to drink. The fountain which attracted particular attention, satisfying that perverse mixture of the grand and the vulgar, is manufactured from a pair of stone breasts. Proud breasts. Breasts rampant, from which spout two jet streams of reviving water. If you were making a documentary film in this location, it would be difficult to resist the accompanying music of Respighi.

I spent the morning of this day in the cool communion

Fountains of the Villa d'Este. Rome

Zeffirelli had promised. I had no profound thoughts. I felt no pressures. I couldn't even claim that I was excited by what I saw. All that I know is that I was in exactly the right place at exactly the right time. One of the few occasions, so far, where a quiet harmony prevailed.

★   ★   ★

I had packed my Hilton bags and toyed, as usual, with the possibilities of sending a card home. I have never really seen the point of it. The space you are given induces immediate paralysis of the 'wish you were here' sort. And no one ever writes 'glad you are not'!

I am similarly disinclined to the use of the camera. Everyone else is snapping. 'Stand a little to your left so that I can get in the Leaning Tower, the Eiffel and Bloody Towers, Blackpool and Trump Tower . . .' Mind you, this sounds a little naive as there is a large, proficient and experienced television crew at my left hand. They provide an excuse for not taking photographs. I provide the reasons.

At the hey-day height of the Grand Tour, it was important for profligate young lords to send progress reports to the heads of the families. I had been reading about the sharpness of an exceptional Roman artist called Batoni. He had a bright little eye to the main chance. He set up his easel in the Piazza Navona which, even in those days, was a hot tourist trap, and he would make a quick charcoal drawing or a more expensive oil, placing you, the traveller, in whatever background you so desired. Thus you could be in the high Alps, or at the foot of Vesuvius, or at the helm of a felucca. More mundanely, you could be in St Peter's Square, or with your profile to the fountains of Navona. Whatever you required. Then you sent the pictures back to the English country seat, despatched at various intervals, whilst you dallied with some red-lipped full-busted courtesan in a suite of Roman rooms. And Mama and Papa, at home, would consider their money to be well spent, and would marvel at the broad European horizons you had surveyed. Not a bad business. Sensible commerce, in fact, in which everyone is suited with the transaction.

I had my portrait drawn in charcoal in the same piazza. It is a ludicrous effort. I look about seventeen years old, and the surprise on my face suggests that I may just have been interfered with by the hand of a mature French lady under the Christmas dinner table. It cost twelve pounds sterling, and I would have been better employed buying six good bottles of Italian frascati.

★   ★   ★

Not sorry to leave Rome. Some kind of nagging begins to develop on the autostrada to Naples. I am on the last lap of my journey. My mind is full of images and my thoughts will probably not be marshalled until I have time to ponder. The nagging springs, I now know, from the realisation that in a week, maybe, all this will be over. I shall have to say goodbye to that little band of people I have travelled with. There are six or seven of us who have learned a lot about each other. How to avoid the electric charges which set off unnecessary quarrels. How to calm anxieties. How to celebrate a particularly happy day. How much sugar in his coffee; how much sleep she needs; what indeed are the low points and high points of everybody's days.

I now believe in biorhythms. I know that I am fairly useless in the early mornings. I know that in the fierce heat of this Italian journey, I do not kick start myself until a glass of cold beer at half-past eleven. I know that I will swear every single day that I do not need to break the activity for lunch and yet, every day, I linger over the table. I know that I cannot have a siesta. There is much too much to see and do. I have learned that, although I find Trades Unions tiresome and often intransigent, I nevertheless breathe a sigh of relief when someone puts a categorical foot down and says that enough is enough. I am alive in the evenings. It is not to do with the sun going down, or the dark, or even, important in my personal case, to do with a more reasonable temperature. It is, quite simply, that I have run up to speed. The batteries are charged, the motor is running. I am cruise-controlled.

And driving past the white reconstruction of Monte Cassino, the hilltop monastery blown off the map by the Allied bombardments, a place now of contemplative silence and slow time, I am saddened by the fact that there is no time to stop there for my customary spiritual fix.

I have never driven into the city of Naples before. I have landed at the airport and been whisked by taxi to the Mergellina, the harbour where you collect the hydrofoil for the off-lying islands of Ischia and Capri. Then I have spent lazy days with the late Sir William Walton OM, of Werneth Hall Road, Oldham and La Mortella, his island paradise in Ischia. It's ten years or slightly more since I conceived a grand plan to bring together two Lancashire musicians in exile. The one was Gracie Fields, of Rochdale and Canzone del Mar, Capri, and the other was William Walton. They were born fifteen miles from each other, the same age; they had lived, fifteen miles from each other, at each end of the Bay of Naples; and one day, as a result of my persistence, this improbable encounter took place in Gracie's restaurant. It was not any kind of musical summit, nor was it a disaster. Both of them seemed pleased. William discovered that 'Sally' was written in the same key as his First Symphony. She said she had a record of it, but didn't play it much. Her gentle husband, Boris Alperovici, struck immediate contact with Susana Walton, William's now-widow, a fiery and opinionated Argentinian lady. It rained all day. When we were leaving to take William and Susana back to Naples and thence to Ischia, Gracie tugged my sleeve to ask me who was paying for lunch. In the subsequent years, I made a natural home for myself with the Waltons; partly due to this vexing question of snobbery, mainly to do with luxurious creature comforts, and the fact that Susana cooked a rich pasta in the carved-out half of a whole Parmesan cheese. When it comes to food, I think I know upon which side my bread is buttered.

William Walton died five years ago and Susana remains a firm friend and, having negotiated the spaghetti complexities of the drive into Napoli Centro, and discovered the spare delights of the Britannia Hotel (Union Jack flying outside), I met the Lady Walton at the quay side. She was to be today's baton bearer.

'My dear chap,' she pronounced upon arrival, 'you look flustered and exhausted.'

'I am. I am. Will you de-fluster me.'

'I will. I will. I am taking you now to Santa Chiara.'

She conducted me to the strangest place, in the heart of the city. I beg you not to yawn or to lose any proper interest when I tell you that it is a monastery. Yet again. More precisely, it is a place of contemplation for nuns, though not, if one is being too precise, a nunnery. We walked into cloisters, rose gardens, by plashy fountains, little benches, medieval wall paintings, and low walls decorated with coloured tiles telling biblical stories and made of Capodimonte faience. You will have to take my word, or Michelin's, that it is a place of immense charm and worth half an hour's foot resting.

The Convent of the Poor Clares was built for a special purpose and one of which Susana Walton relishes the retelling.

'You see, the noble families of Naples used to put their unmarried daughters into this place. When the head of the particular family found that there was no one noble or important enough left to marry a particular daughter, she was more or less confined to a beautiful virginity within these walls. They brought their ladies-in-waiting, their servants, their father-confessors. But they were not allowed out.' (This last sentence she speaks in sombre capital letters.)

'Were they imprisoned?'

'No one called it imprisonment. They were devoted to the service of God. Except that it was the family who devoted them, not they themselves. There was no counterpart in society fit enough to suit them. Their fathers (now we are down to nailing the villain) would never allow them to marry beneath them!'

Some of the painted tiles are of a particularly secular nature, depicting scenes which are not altogether spiritual.

'Of course. These proud cloistered women wanted to be reminded of some – only some – of the pleasures they had been forced to abandon. Here is a man pressing grapes – *man – pressing – grapes*. A luscious physical trinity. Do you know what I mean?'

'Yes, Lady Walton, one knows exactly what one means!'

As if to provide the strongest possible confirmation, our conversation was disturbed by the unexpected sight of a bride and her groom, with their attendants, making a slow progress through this quiet place. It is, apparently, now a tradition that a new bride be photographed in such holy circumstance, before she leaves for honeymoon and the rest of a shackled life. And all the ghostly bells of Santa Chiara ring in a clang of jubilation and sorrow to mark this change in the life of a young woman.

Susana Walton is a woman very much of this world, even though she keeps one eye clearly centred upon the nourishing traditions of the old.

We left the cloisters and went to the market in the Spacca-Napoli – the Roman street which cuts through the heart of the city. It is noisy, narrow, busy, slightly threatening, wholly diverting. For ten pounds sterling you can buy a smart black frock with a St Laurent label stitched to the inside. For another ten pounds you can buy a pair of supposedly Gucci shoes. The names have been changed to protect the guilty.

There are no questions asked. It would be foolish to make any kind of investigation. Look there. A man in dark glasses with very oily black hair standing in the shade at the back of the busy shop might well call in the mates to deal with a tiresome customer.

'Why are these handbags so cheap when they appear to have been made in Florence,' I start to ask, but my confident questing voice trails into a whisper when I see the dark force behind the counter.

'Not wise to ask too many questions, darling,' advises the worldy-wise widow Walton, from the corners of a tight mouth.

In so many aspects, this is the most foreign city I have encountered upon the travels. The air of Arabia is not too far away. On half-a-dozen days of the year the winds carry sand over the Mediterranean and plonk great dollops of it on to cars and washing lines. The air is also full of the feel of 'dealing'. I don't know what the right word is here. It's not so much 'dealing' as 'bartering', and it's not so much to do with barter as with the very process of existence. Three sheep may equal one cow. Three bicycles may equal one secondhand Fiat. It needs no more than an ordinary human computer to make that kind of mathematical balance. Here, however, you get the sense that lives are involved too. And they make a churning mess of anybody's mechanical calculations.

There is a lot of smuggling and drug-trafficking and, without being too precise about it, a certain amount of trade in human bodies. I do not mean prostitution, which is as prosperous an occupation here as in any throbbing city. I mean something darker and simpler. Like buying children, or servants, or slaves.

I happened to meet a journalist who told me of a certain regularity of practice concerning the local priest. This father of the church is in thrall to the contrabandisti, the pirates who smuggle in any commodity worth their while and their energy. They are marked men. Particularly in the past year when the law, such as it is, has tightened around the freer spirits of piracy. The contrabandisti dare not land upon the shore now. They have to make arrangements for cargo to be lifted off and sorted through other channels. Sometimes, by natural means, one of the crew dies at sea and the proper Catholic obsequies must be observed. This is a powerful Catholic land, and sea. The contrabandisti have their hooks firmly upon one particular priest. They send a flashing light to signal a request for his presence. He makes his own arrangements for embarkation and meets the boat at sea. He says prayers for the departed soul. The crew make the sign of the cross. The body is committed to the warm waves and the priest is returned in safety to his home. There are no questions asked. Expediency is an efficient master and makes no undue moral demands.

The patron saint of the city of Naples is San Gennaro, St Januarius. Twice a year, on the first Saturday in May and on the nineteenth of September, in his own church, there is celebrated the Feast of the Miracle of this same St Gennaro. The Cardinal Archbishop and the Mayor of the City, each privately possessing a silver key, process to the high altar, and then on and behind to the silver reliquary, where there is a phial of this saint's dried blood. The Cathedral is crowded. The Archbishop cradles the phial in his holy hands and makes prayer and supplication to God, to give the people of this city the optimistic sign of liquefaction.

Quite by chance, being shown the restoration to stone-work and the pictures in this Cathedral, by Mirella Barracco, who spends her days and most of her nights persuading people to conserve the damaged glories of this city, I happened to meet a concerned businessman sitting in a choir stall and looking up at the workers on a ceiling scaffold. The Baronessa Barracco told me his name, which I have forgotten. But she said that he was a sort of Sainsbury, a grocer who had made his money, and was now making proper philanthropic use of it, diverting huge amounts to help to restore the cracks of minor earthquakes. I said 'Good day', and talked to him about the miracle of the liquefaction.

Under any other circumstance, you would use the word 'hard-headed', as in 'businessman'. This is the surprise he offered me:

'Last year I was the guest of the Cardinal Archbishop of Naples and I was sitting up there next to him, and I saw him take out the phial of crusted blood. It was dry. And he kept rotating it in his hands, and you could see, easily see, a level of liquid developing in the glass.'

'What, do you think, is the explanation?'

'There is no explanation . . . except I felt a great personal joy. Joy which you feel when something immensely magnificent is happening against the rules.'

'Does it ever *not* happen?'

'Yes, and it is a sad day for this city. In 1980 the blood did not liquefy and then we had this terrible earthquake. I do not have answers. I have questions. Is it coincidence; is it a sign; is it an omen? The liquefaction did not occur just before the refinery exploded.'

'Are the Neapolitans . . . are you . . . superstitious?'

Pause.

'In these things, the borders between faith and superstition and belief are so very difficult to define.'

'Can I see the phial?'

'No. Only if you have a key, and there are only two, and the Cardinal has the one and the Mayor, who is about to change, has the other. The Mayor of Naples, incidentally, is often a communist but he always comes here with his key!'

Knowing, I thought to myself, which side his wafer is buttered on!

When the original Grand Tourists came to Naples, they

sneaked into the back of the Cathedral to witness this spectacle, and when, in those days, the miracle didn't work, the Cardinal would scream about the possible presence of a Protestant spirit constricting the free agency of Catholic energy.

Energy is a combination of the faith of the people and their enthusiasm and their desire and their will to see this thing come to pass. 'It is *very* important and very touching. They want a miracle. They want a sign,' said Signor Sainsbury. Why is it that very successful grocers become so civilised and so sophisticated in their thinking? So literate and so liberal?

'When I saw the liquefaction, I saw it through tears in my own eyes. I was grateful.'

There are, I thought again, more things in heaven and this teeming city than are dreamt of in the philosophy of the package tourist.

You hear such dreadful things about Naples. About noise and disease, and dirt, and murder, and thieving, and traders who will smile and rip you off. You hear about pollution and the pernicious presence of the American navy. About pimps and prostitutes. About decay and the Mafia, crooked policemen and, were it possible, even more crooked politicians.

And yet.

That which is absolutely undeniable is an almost electric energy. The same kind of instant intoxication which you feel in New York City. In which other historical city, for heaven's sake, would a voluptuous woman called Emma Hamilton, married to a vulcanologist, artist and plenipotentiary, Sir William Hamilton, have provided afternoon tea at the Villa Emma, accompanied by a little light music, and then a session in the drawing-room where she would strike almost naked poses in classic attitudes? They say she had big innocent eyes and a volcanic body. Then she met the Admiral Lord Nelson, and became, eventually, a part of Hollywood's mythology. She died, a fat alcoholic, in Calais, in hiding from creditors who were chasing her.

No place I have so far encountered on this journey breeds so much documented mythology. Zeffirelli explained Vesuvius. And it is there, in grand glowering conical dominance.

Just before I arrived, the Naples Football Team, led by

Diego Maradona (who, unlike the Pope, will not grant an audience), won the Italian League Cup. Instead of beating the hell out of each other, the supporters, and all those who had interests in other clubs, poured money into a fund which paid an engineer and his company a fortune. With this money he discovered a way in which to line the inside rim of Vesuvius with a blue and white gunpowder. These are the colours of Naples. When the winning goal was scored, the volcano burst into flames and smoke. And into the night spilled the benign fire and light, sending the reflected message of victory up to the clouds and mirroring this vast triumph in the darkened waters of the Bay.

And I missed it.

But on the last night of this very Grand Tour, I went to join the celebrations upon the feast day of Santa Maria del Carmine. You would not consider it worth the détour. The presence of the church is not loudly advertised. Nothing much happens, apart from a brass band and a booze-up, and a rickety wooden stand which contains the local dignitaries sitting like rows of pompous eggs on a rack. The local postman invited me to watch the fireworks from his family balcony, in a little flat overlooking the square, next to the docks.

It was a scene lifted straight from Eduardo da Fillipo and not too precisely directed by Franco Zeffirelli. Lots of wine. Lots of children. Lots of black plastic sofas and vases full of pale pink tulips, each containing a little electric light. Huge bowls of sticky sweets. Men sweating. Women with hairy armpits in tight tricel. Couples making a furtive embrace in a corner. Newspaper pictures of the Pope in Brazil stuck on the wall with Blu Tack. Via di Coronazione, Hilda Ogden, Mavis Riley, all the old familiar faces. Granny Harty would have loved all this. My mother would too. So many surfaces to mop. Masterful gentlemen putting their wet-bottomed glasses of beer onto highly polished glass-topped tables. Crumbs to pick up from the gaudy carpet. Bottle tops to be placed precisely into specially ordered bin-liners, and no ashtray allowed to overflow.

Do you wonder that I felt that, in some very strange way, I had come home?

At ten o'clock, the most absurdly touching final manife-

The last night. Fireworks. Naples

station of this whole glorious journey. 'Watch. Watch. Ecco. Ecco.'

From the belfry of the church, right opposite our family balcony, came an electric star on a wire. The wire ran from the top of the church to a little hut in the square. The star descended slowly and in awesome silence. It lit upon the little house where it was mechanically hooked, upon the picture of Santa Maria, Mary, the Madonna. Gradually, and still in profound silence, the star dragged the gaudy and primitive face of Santa Maria up into the coal black sky. Vulgar naked electric bulbs made a twentieth-century frame around her image. The star eventually took home the saint and, at the moment she was lodged back safely in her tower, the whole building exploded in a fantasy of fireworks. Huge sparkling waterfalls of fire. Catherine wheels, rockets of joy, Roman candles – and the band blasted its brass at the crowd, and the crowds crossed themselves and cried.

And so, for the first time, did I.

★　　★　　★

INDEX

ACKNOWLEDGEMENTS

I couldn't have made this journey without Pat Heald. She is my other half, and could, in all probability, have written this book had I keeled over half-way through the journey. It would be impudent of me to measure the help she has given me.

Derek Bailey directed me, in almost every sense. Not simply turn left, turn right. He it was who said, 'You are being self-indulgent, grand, silly or snobbish.' Even when I thought I was right, I had to face the awesome fact that he knew better.

John Rooney played the part of John the Baptist, rough places plain and all that, to handsome advantage. His help is not quantifiable. His cheerfulness, and his grace, are.

I wandered through Europe with a motley band. Emanuele Pasquale opened the most private of doors, even when they had odd numbers, supplied by Jenny Rivarola. Norma Howson did the laundry, and, in the middle of the Palio in Siena, wandered off to buy a cheese grater. She also discovered that she was in the same school class as Sister Scholastica. They had a private laugh about that.

The television crew, who shadowed and framed me, became loving brothers. Graham Veevers, my camera man, offered the minimal criticism, but when he was disappointed, pushed his tongue in his cheek. Mick Farr spent his spare time polishing his steel frames the clearer to read Proust and Ezra Pound. Alan Parker gave up, half-way through, and said to me, one night, he'd be better off married. And he is. Dennis Cartwright, who looks like Father Christmas, fixed many a microphone to me and to others. Sometimes he had to explain to people like the Pope and Armani, exactly who I was. 'Well' he said, in his rubicund enthusiasm, 'He's "the turn". They bring him on when there's nobody else. He's a nightmare. But we quite like him.'

And I like them.

Hugh Williams was the man who launched this hesitant craft, and Ian Squires wore the Admiral's uniform.

If I have not included everybody, like Jane Val Baker, they surely know me well enough to forgive me. I have to stop now, otherwise I shall start to cry again, and Jane Birt's lovely pictures will be all smudged.